"In these lyric essays, Kathryn Winogra[d] wife, and writer, wilding her selves again and traction Winograd gets by pinning emotion, whether alive now or in me[...] What a tough essayist–and tender voice–the West has been waiting for all these years, ever since the ancient ones first arrived."

—THOMAS LARSON, AUTHOR OF **The Sanctuary of Illness, The Saddest Music Ever Written** AND **The Memoir and the Memoirist**

"Winograd finds the most unlikely containers for the most urgent subjects. How does one reconcile, in the natural world, science and faith? Eyes, mind, and heart wide open, Winograd shows us what she can hold in her hand—shotguns, bird eggs, mushroom spores—and tilts our chins up to study the night sky . . . The very best books invent their own genres and Winograd's *Phantom Canyon* has done just that. The shimmering syntax, the metaphor, the way the patterned images add up to something that wasn't there before—that's the lyric. But there's also a story here. *Phantom Canyon* is a page-turner, a collection of lyric essays you won't be able to put down. As a writer, teacher, mother, daughter, and survivor, I needed this book. You do, too."

—JILL CHRISTMAN, AUTHOR OF **Darkroom: A Family Exposure**

"In *Phantom Canyon* Kathryn Winograd takes her place among America's most celebrated writers—Thoreau and Annie Dillard come immediately to mind— who turn to the violence and beauty of nature to spark deeper understandings of the human community, and of the body and mind. Winograd adds to the mix her own insistence to confront even the most violent personal trauma—her own experience being raped as a child. For Kathryn Winograd the lyrical imagination, spiritual healing, and the love of beauty everywhere around us, come most fully alive only through recognizing also the harsher realities of the human condition. In a 'long bow to the earth and to the fragile self,' Winograd offers us the fullness and frailty of her own life, the natural world and the people she loves."

—STEPHEN HAVEN, AUTHOR OF **The Last Sacred Place in North America** AND **The River Lock: One Boy's Life along the Mohawk**.

"Kathryn Winograd's *Phantom Canyon* is a compelling collection. Here is the lyric essay at its most perceptive and powerful. I admire the insight and intelligence of the essays, the magnetic and masterful drive of the language, and above all the aching honesty that infuses every page."

—ROBERT ROOT, AUTHOR OF **Happenstance** AND **Postscripts: Retrospections on Time and Place**

PHANTOM CANYON

Essays of Reclamation

KATHRYN WINOGRAD

A Division of Samizdat Publishing Group

CONUNDRUM PRESS A Division of Samizdat Publishing Group.
PO Box 1279, Golden, Colorado 80402

Cover design by Sonya Unrein.
Cover sketch by Jeff Knubley.

For information, email info@conundrum-press.com.

ISBN: 978-1-938633-24-9

Library of Congress Cataloging-in-Publication Data is available upon request.

Conundrum Press books may be purchased with bulk discounts for educational, business, or sales promotional use. For information please email: Conundrum Press online: conundrum-press.com

To my mother and father with love always
To Leonard, always

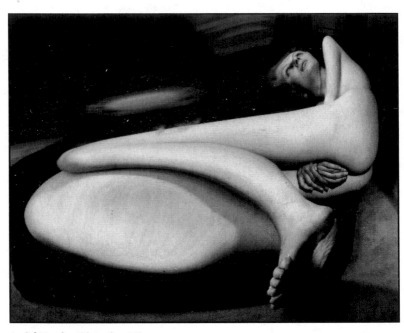

André Kertész, Distortion #40
©Estate of André Kertész/Higher Pictures.

On André Kertész's Distortion #40

Call her daughter as if this were not the self distorted here, as if some she-god were not long secreted in your valved and unquiet heart, the small stirrings of her, who birthed you, a motion now, a dream of motion.

The man the photographer morphs this woman into all she is not. She is the detail almost forgotten here—dead-centered the mirror's distortion itself or its symbols of distortion, its squares and loops of the body, its triangles of shoulders—as if the holy shapes to quiet us, as she is quiet.

Girl? Woman? Mother? She is too young to be a mother, we think. How small the buttocks. How unwomanly pressed against the frame, against our downward pull of gravity willing her into form, into formlessness, into what she has named herself: "Virgin forest, bird-like reflection, emptiness."

What disturbs us are the hands, there is so much to the hands, fingers multiplying curves, multiplying—a bouquet of hands crowning out of the weak mouth of the vagina, what she has clasped as if in prayer: a rosary of flesh, a rose, a sea creature climbing godly out of the frail wall of her body.

Contents

Dark Skies

It is fall, past the autumnal equinox. I drive, almost sick with fear, the world outside my window telescoped down to a pinhole of light, "a wandering star"—Jupiter? Mars? Saturn? I cannot tell—suspended above the roadside. My headlights carve the landscape into a verticality of ghost aspen and fencepost, while a fleeting horizon of barbed wire holds fast the vegetating night over Phantom Canyon.

I don't know this dark. I am a woman of light trespass, of stellar extinction. On the satellite's map of the lit world, I live on the urban lip of a cosmos, a constelled city glittering against the void of mountain and eastern plain. The few nights when I remember to, I stand at the mouth of my garage counting the scarce stars that quicken above the schoolyard before the streetlight's annihilating glow. I am one of the world's half population for whom night is not night, but a gradation, a half moon of light never waning.

Yet this is what I wanted, building our cabin here, instead of in some skier's floodlit paradise, here among the gravel roads and the wheel ruts of Teller County where I might someday, like Thoreau, hear a wind bearing "terrestrial music" through the lonely cattle bones and the wild iris.

Behind me, Colorado Springs is a small backwash of sky glow. I am forty-seven and I have never once been alone like this. I force myself to look left, to crane my head against the side window and see the stars, brilliant white, glide into view. I am traveling beneath strange dark skies and I think it is the old memories that crush me—the unholy dark beyond the primitive flame, the unholy men who take girls deep into the mythic earth, their mothers still weeping in their dark veils of winter. Left at the cattle corral. Then left past the iron cattle guard. The ruins of old miners' cabins and settler homes flick past, and I see as if for the first time the men and women who huddled together in sod houses, in covered wagons, in log cabins with tiny window slits, while the great whale of the night swallowed them.

My car lights sweep across the endless, empty meadows, until finally they reach the stones of our cabin. Soon all will be light. The stove will burn white hot with scrap wood and the radio will hiss with jazz and distant cities and airwaves. Slowly the air will heat, take on weight, cover my face with its hands until my eyes shut, while the wind drafts in the stove pipe, sucks spark and ember, the tiniest shreds of smoke into the night sky hovering unseen some thirty feet above me. And I will stare into the back window to watch the life I thought never to have— reversed, backward, the dream of myself reflected against a dark netherworld until piece by piece, fear sheds from me like some mother of pearl.

I open the car door, ready to run, the key to the cabin door poised in my hand. Darkness is overwhelming, immense, a black shroud between the world and me. What do we miss in a place of no real night, a place of misdirected streetlights, of scattering aerosols, of sign illuminations, and diurnal moths battering at our lighted windows?

Silence. Wind. Coyote. A longhorn's faint bawling in the

November dearth of grass. Slowly, my eyes adapt. The air pales. Snow beneath the implacable pines silvers like the metallic salts of some film developing. A thread of the moon curves in the east, the whole sky filled with the bent river of the Milky Way. I count the far single lights of my neighbors scattered down to the Arkansas River Valley and its thousand lights of a thousand small cities.

This is why you came, I tell myself, and step slowly into the dark.

The strange woman buries you deep in fire
and works grief and bitter sorrow

—Homeric Hymn 2 to Demeter

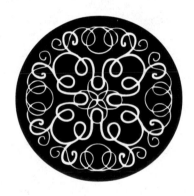

Phantom Mares

Thou shalt not pass over this heap and this pillar unto me, for harm.

—Genesis 31:52

When my daughters were ten, I took them to a horse farm on the eastern plains of Colorado to watch semen collected from a stallion.

To protect the brood mare in estrus, the breeder uses a "phantom mare," a sawhorse contraption of wood and padding that the stallion mounts, the handler directing the stallion's semen, whiter than a man's, I've heard, into a collection bag attached to an AV, an artificial vagina made of sterile latex and a hard-shelled water jacket that can be heated or frozen.

We drove past Platteville and a fledgling river I could not name and a cemetery called *Mizpah*, the Lord's "watchtower," the Bible says, where an early 1900s eastern plains woman I only learned about now lay interred amongst the prairie dog holes and the slumbering, winter-den rattlesnakes she once slaughtered, a hundred and forty in an afternoon, and then sewed into a dress of skin.

I don't know why this woman matters now, or why I keep thinking of her slitting the delicate skin at the snake's throat, carefully cutting through the fibrous fascia, then gripping the long cool bodies, snake after snake, to peel each skin down to the chambered rattle so that she too might wear it. But I do.

★ ★ ★

Sometimes on fall afternoons in Ohio, the humidity burnt clear and the universe peeled open as if to some blue and reachable heaven, my father would lure Trigger, our wild-eyed, barn-soured gelding from the bottom fields with sweet corn, to mount him like a god we feared would fall.

Trigger was the horse we kids half-feared, the one that once reared so far skyward he flipped over, foaming and sweat-dark. Our aunt, experienced horsewoman that she was, could barely untangle herself from the stirrups before the saddle horn dug full force into the dirt, Trigger pinned on his back for a heart-stilling moment, then kicking, twisting himself to his hooves and thundering past us into the open barn.

Even on good days, he fought beneath us, my brother and sister and me, in the imperviousness of youth, racing this gelding bareback through the plowed corn fields, our constricted thighs coagulated with sweat and horse hair and fly spray as we hung on hard to his mane, squeezed our legs tight around his rib cage, our tail bones banging the hard ellipses of his spine until we clucked him into air, clucked him into a divine thunder I thought we could surely hold onto forever. But we couldn't.

★ ★ ★

I want to tell you that this is about healing now, that this is why I could take my daughters at such a young age to some breeding barn, some stud farm on the eastern plains of Colorado, to watch the artificial insemination of a mare, because when I was their age my father, Doc Burt, the farmers called him, could swing his leg over Trigger's back, thump down into the saddle seat, round-shouldered and pot-bellied, and kick the white–eyed Trigger into a half-lurching trot to make house calls on the neighboring farmers who claimed my father could save them.

But I'm not sure what this means now, how anyone can save anyone else, much less a father save a daughter, and I keep thinking about the woman I once saw through a half-opened door when I was a candy striper at the hospital where my father sent his patients, this woman leaning over a slack-eyed, head-shorn girl, my age, I thought, victim of a horse fall, I found out later.

"Here, Jane," the woman kept saying. "Do you hear this? Do you hear this, my Jane?" And she jangled a silver bell at her daughter's white unhearing ear.

★ ★ ★

The eastern plains woman carried her child on horseback to a pond to collect wounded ducks from a hunter. When she dismounted to lift the gate and open it, the first snake slid out from beneath the prairie grass and she shot it. And then a second slid out, aroused by the bullet's vibration, and then a third, and then another, and another until finally, without bullets, she beat the rattlesnakes dead one after another with a post until her hands bled, a hundred and forty snakes coming out to do her harm, to do her child harm.

In the book of Genesis, when Laban, father of Leah and Rachel, meets Jacob the deceiver, he says, "These daughters *are* my daughters, these children *are* my children," and he builds a heap of stones, a mizpah, a covenant between his daughters and Jacob so that no harm may be done to them. I'll tell you I wanted to breed our dainty Arabian, drinker of wind, flesh of the Fertile Crescent, only to the purest bloodlines, and so we came to this barn of her birth to learn this process, not because

I kept thinking about my daughters, mine, so soon to the age of thirteen, or of myself at that age—already raped, already marked—as if to show them this, this sex in this way, might stave them from some harm.

The barn manager, native of the eastern European country that the grandparents of my sloe-eyed daughters fled from so long ago, showed us first his home, his self-portrait in Napoleonic uniform gracing the fireplace mantel, and, beneath it, his tender, long-necked orchids floating flushed and tethered. Back in the barn, he pulled a long tube marked in millimeters from a small refrigerator.

"This is semen," he said, waving it in front of my daughters. "Semen."

★ ★ ★

Down the gravel lane past the fallen gravestones, down past the aluminum farm gate we did not yet close most nights, down Goshen-Murdoch Road my father would ride, yelling back at us kids to watch out for the beer bottles shattered in the broken grass we tripped through. This was our part of the ritual too, running in the road ditch to catch up with him, half praying for no car to thunder down the blind curve of the hill and run into him, his elbows flapping in the air as he rode up the hill to the old one-room schoolhouse where Jack lived. Jack was the fast driving, hard drinking bad boy that his younger brother, whom I would soon try to slap on the school bus, still wept for—Jack paralyzed years then, a drunk in a wheelchair only my father, you must be thinking now, could save.

But Jack is dead. And so is my father, grinning slightly now as he chews a stem of grass beneath his sweat stained straw hat, still sidling over to talk soybeans to the farmers we rented our fields to those many years ago, my mother reminding me in the lore of my father of another city-boy drawn into the fields as my father was, once bruising his leg while plowing, and thinking nothing of it until he fell dead in the field, still plowing, a blood clot passing through his veins to his heart and lodging there.

"If only he had talked to your father," my mother says, shaking her head. "Your father would have known what to do." But he didn't. Not ever.

★ ★ ★

Long light triggered this mare into estrus and the handlers led her back and forth, tail-flagging past the screaming stallion strutting in his stall, the barn manager depositing my daughters and me on bales of hay to watch in safety as his handlers finally led the stallion, rigid and flaring, through the barn to where a placid "jump" mare waited patiently in a headstall to deceive him into mounting this phantom mare of wood and padding.

I don't remember what my daughters said or did, but already I was thinking "no," already I was thinking how wrong this was, how helpless to sit here and watch with my young daughters this stallion mounting this phantom mare, how what harms you most always seems to come down to an image—the stranger leaning over you in winter leaves, or the mare your father "pasture breeds" to a borrowed stallion, his barring you from the barn cellar windows and you bewildered in that cacophony squealing out of the same barn where you had watched your first cow slaughtered—shot in the head, dragged by chains to the barn door and hoisted up bleeding, dead-eyed, fly-heavy until the neighbor butcher plunged his knife through the belly skin—ah, there is that woman and her snakes—and floated the hide off in one piece from the shiny sheathes of muscle and fat, the ground beneath your child feet turned black with a blood you cannot wash from your shoes.

★ ★ ★

Sometimes I think it's about the sexual or the celestial. The dirty jokes about girls and horses or the "free" liberated women waxing poetic about the sinew and muscle along the high spine of the horse and the jutting withers the cunt embraces. Or the horse is all divinity—Epona the Celtic goddess, "Great Mare" of the equine, leading the wandering soul between earth and spirit.

But I want to think it's about power, how a young girl can take a mammal of a thousand pounds or more, secure it with a small lash of leather, a metal bit, a small rag of blanket and overcome it, usurp it in a way, but in love, too: the sugar cube in the flat of the hand, the soft seeking muzzle, the warm breath on the wrist, and the secret thrill of the teeth grazing the taut skin of the giving palm.

I remember, later, riding Trigger past the fence line into my neighbors' pastures. I think I was past healing, already afraid to walk through the gate alone as if the fences of my father's farm encircled me like some mizpah, some covenant I relinquished with my passing, unlatching the wire gate from the fencepost, and drawing the horse through, each time with that little uncertainty of whether I could get up again, grasp the dry tuft of mane hair, or ever lever my hand above a loin and leap in faith upward.

★ ★ ★

So this must be about the horse then, not my father, or even my mother, who could not save me, who loved me I realize now only in helplessness, the way I love my own, the way Laban loved the lesser daughter Leah, who was weak-eyed, and so gave her veiled, in secret, to Jacob, despite the covenant stones between them. Jacob did not want her, and would not. And it's not just this horse, or the little Arabian I never did breed, but the horse named Grace, the one long after my father died that I hauled

out of the shadows of the Sangre de Cristo mountains in a borrowed trailer, my twin daughters thirteen-years-old then and
weeping in the back of the car because Grace is shit-stained and
Grace is half-starved, a bony rack they had not yet learned to
want, but that I had.

★ ★ ★

Trigger would go where I wanted, older now, though sometimes he bent his broad neck downward, twisted his head toward
my knee to gaze at me, as if I should let him wander freely,
divine envoy leading the aimless me to a destiny I had learned
to fear, the clear glass of his eye like a crystal ball I could not
look through. I wanted to believe the myths, how the horse in
its great love for me would save me, balanced so carefully along
his heart girth, and run me from the strangers still haunting my
neighbor's woods, run me untouchable over the cold stones of
a creek bed and the gullies where a small girl's body could lie
hidden for years in the hoar frost. But I couldn't.

★ ★ ★

"I can heal her," I thought, and so this is where the healing comes
in, you must think, this father's daughter, daughter of Eve like
the eastern plains snake woman, dirt farmer long forsaken of any
garden and wrapping herself in the skin of what has harmed her.

It was near evening and my daughters had to deworm this
mare, push the syringe and its sloppy contents along her teeth
and inject it, her tongue trying to push it out, block it from her
throat, from swallowing it. They had taught her to rear and I
remember thinking how like ash she rose up on her hind feet, as
if my daughters' small whip lifted her, and later the woman at
the horse rescue who said she had seen nearly everything, blaming the human always, blaming my daughters, me, for this mare

striking out so viciously at them, saying someone has taught her to rear as if all the sin were always our own.

There is something biblical here, the phantom mare and the man I took my daughters to when they were so young, and the snake and all its venom, and Laban saying to Jacob, "If you afflict my daughters," as if he himself would not, and, finally, Grace, balancing here, black against the blackening evening, while a woman who has been hurt wraps her breasts in scales, holds them out to the children she feeds, even when they have been conceived in love, and says, "Here is my milk and its little poisons."

Bear of my Girlhood

When I first saw it, when at last the bear of my girlhood unlocked itself from the stone shadows and I could see the fine frosted hairs of its crooked dog legs, I could not leave it. Here was that dream from the flowered room of my Midwestern girlhood, my parents sleeping so far from me down the darkened hallway, and the bear rising from the sleeping hollows of my veins until I staggered wounded from my bed to crawl between my parents, to train my heart to their slow, blinded ones.

In Ohio, we like to say nothing is wild. Not the geese scattered across the gold rind of autumn, not the deer hushed in trembling mist nor the Black Angus dotting the green fields like ruptured earth. This is what my parents wanted—to believe we lived safely amid the neat pin tucks of cornfields and fenced timothy where the huge blurred shadows of poplar and oak dip down through the soft silver of evening. And for the whole of my childhood, this is what I wanted to believe too, as if what I feared had been only imaginary or elusive: the copperhead curled about the leaf mat like Eve's snake, the barn bat pricking the sleeping cow's hide.

When I moved to the West, everything changed—that knife-cut of light over the red bones of the mountains, those wild creatures my parents still warned me of each time I returned home, the names rolling from their tongues like exotic language: puma, lynx, coyote, grizzly. No, I told them again and again. No. I have never seen one. I have never stepped through the wild mountains alone, never alone stood beneath a fierce blue sky, listened alone to some far tundra wind singing the dark pines. I am still your daughter, I told them, who once crept between your sleeping bodies.

When I first spent the night on the mountain's back, it was with my husband. I could not sleep. I could not hear enough, I could not see enough, and, all night, that bear of my girlhood hovered over our tent, its claws extended, ripping me again and again into black air. But then, slowly, I learned what it was to walk in quiet, alone under a solitary moon, my husband's shadow barely there through the trees against a small slow fire burning.

When finally I saw this bear, I did not expect it. I stood half-dreaming among the lunar rocks and pine oak. And then, all at once, the hairs on my neck rose, and suddenly, as if I were walking upon the cool paper husks of rattlers, their dreams winter and poison, my heart woke, no longer my parents', no longer blind to such wild beauty.

The dog hammered at her leash. Deer froze in the pines. The sky went dark. Rain fell. I swelled out my great weight, stood taller, stepped into my other body, large-boned and fleshy where there is no sweetness, no girlhood to deny the truth of.

The bear balanced on a rock like a circus bear and watched me back out of the dark world. From the blue caves of snow it had risen, all winter its body sleeping, pulled out of the wind's tick, out of the sun's pendulous turn, this bear, I imagined, mother like me now, that birth in such sleep painless until the lighted spring unclasped us.

In the Midwest, my father bulldozed a pond out of a cornfield when I was my daughters' age and this is where we once stood at a moon-rim of childhood waters. My daughters had returned home with me, and we left my parents' to walk past fescue and clover, hoping to find the gold-eyed frog or the dark thumbnail of tadpole, toys of my childhood.

Have you seen one, my parents had already asked. *Have you?* And I had not yet answered, everything unchanged, I thought, but me—this Midwestern dream, my parents who wanted nothing more of my whole life than to protect me who was no longer theirs.

A dollop of water burst into the air. A dark ring of water trembled.

"There," my daughters shouted, "a frog!" and the tell-tale bubbles popped against the green moss where the slight moons of deer tracks indented the wet mud and dragonflies sparked the evening air.

"Get a net, Mommy," one of my daughters pled, and I turned to start toward the barn, to leave my children alone in Ohio beneath a sky I once called soft as blue china. But then I stopped, my heart so blinded, so never my own.

Guns, Knives, and the Amazon Warrior Princess

I hold the .38 special in my hand. For this gun show, a plastic "twistee" rivets the trigger into benign rigidity, and I stare down its snub nose.

I want a gun.

I like to think I come to this realization through a maze of fact and myth. Fact: my daughter sees a mountain lion in the rocks above our newly built cabin, 9,600 feet above nothing. Fact: we find bear claw marks slashed into a blue bird nest ten feet up in a hollowed aspen. Fact: a four-year-old neighbor wandering too far from her parents in the dense wood calls out: "Scary dog, Mommy, scary dog" and later points to the lion in Disney's *The Lion King*. Myth: our mountain neighbor, Chuck, of the yurt and the folkloric drug raves that once sprawled over our mountain meadows, tells us the tale of a woman on Shelf Road in Phantom Canyon attacked by a grizzly—a bear not seen in Colorado for decades.

"Her arm," he pauses dramatically, "peeled from its socket."

But it's none of this. An elderly drifter in the Georgia mountains has murdered a young woman who was hiking with her dog.

★ ★ ★

Why this news story, one of countless reports of young girls murdered, has sent me here to this gun show and its sea of happy men, I do not know. I live but a mile from Columbine High School. My daughters were second graders at a nearby elementary school on the day of that massacre. They were herded into the school gymnasium by teachers well-trained in anticipation of what for us before then was the unimaginable. The teachers papered their classroom windows dark. They chained the hall doors on the inside.

"Big fire," my daughters said to Leonard when he finally made it through the shrieking emergency vehicles and the long wakes of parental cars to sign them out—this "fire" was the only reason my daughters could fathom for spending the morning locked in a gymnasium. Now each morning, they pull into the Columbine parking lot for school, the words I mouth to the closing garage door trailing after them like little prayer flags.

But I am torn. Before this old man, this sixty-year-old drifter whom I would have stopped to chat with on that mountain trail, whose dog would have played with my dog, who kidnapped the young woman close in age to my daughters for three days, and only then decapitated her, before this man, I thought only of the animal and what gun I might buy to protect myself and my daughters in the wilds around our new cabin—a surprised sow or a mountain lion scouring the snow for rabbit. Not what I might buy to shoot a man.

★ ★ ★

Myth: nice women don't carry guns.

I've had knives. My first was long and lean, a thin, slightly mottled metal sharpened to splay the pink flesh of fish from the delicate arc of vertebrae and body bone. My father said I should catch trout in the mountain lakes to eat, so Leonard bought me this knife, sheathed in cheap leather. I kept it in a fishing bag at first, bringing it out only when I trolled the snowmelt with the wooly buggers and crappies the fish ignored. But then a few times bivouacking up between deserted switchbacks in the gloom of lodge pole pine, I slid the knife into the side pocket of my trousers, as if its thin blade could save me. At night, in the lit bubble of our tent, beneath the circling moon, I would lay with it, my fingers curled around its placid leather as I listened to the deafening stillness of the tundra, and our dog growled.

When I began to hike alone, my husband bought me a larger knife with a leather loop sewn to its case that I could thread my belt through. This one had an elegant curve—like the knives Hollywood pirates teethe. To unholster it, I unsnapped a leather strap that secured the blade, my finger practicing that quick upward flick so many times during my walks alone that the leather stretched, grew lean with my worrying.

What did I imagine I would do with this knife? A charging black bear. A cougar stalking me downwind. An old man smiling. Would I thrust its blade into the living, warm body, beat my head against the ground as if I were some beseeching emissary of Hades trained to hold that balanced weight in my hand, slip those last coins beneath the tongues of my dead before sending them off into the far forgetting?

I think of the Amazon women, myth or fact, sung by Homer and Virgil, those warrior women cleaving their right breasts off for the sake of the bow's fit, their left breasts uncut for the suckling of their young, and of the Amazon princess Penthesilea who lead those thousands into Grecian wars, "a maid clashing with men," until Achilles' spear pierced her above the heart.

Could I be these women and kill?

"I would rather die than own a gun," a friend tells me, her sister dead of a self-inflicted gunshot wound.

★ ★ ★

I rub my finger over the shiny snout of this .38. Years back, I dated the son of a Midwestern deputy. The deputy, his father, would throw the evening meal across the kitchen floor if it were not to his liking. My boyfriend kept a large gun, "a magnum," he said, under his bed to protect himself against the possible midnight rampages of his older brother, whom I only knew through family stories as a half-crazed specter of schizophrenia. I remember sleeping fitfully in that bed like the delicate princess of a hundred mattresses, bruised and aching above the single pea. Only this pea was metal and deadly. The few times I held the gun at the firing range under that flat Iowan sky, my hands shook with its weight as I squinted down to the bullseye. But it was all sham and flirtatious play: me nervous and silly, coddled affectionately at the firing range until, finally succumbing to its bruising kickback, I gave the gun up.

The man at the gun show who owns this .38 stares at me. I like it. I like all of it—the show, this gun, his stare at a graying woman who fingers speculatively what might have killed another.

"Bear?" I ask him. "Mountain lion?" I do not ask him my real question.

Man?

★ ★ ★

I think of my father, ten years now beneath the Murdoch cemetery in Ohio where honeysuckle and birds weave the quiet each time I visit him. He nicknamed me "Cautious Keekee," emblem of the long years of thumb-sucking that pushed my crossbite straight, the long years of stuffed rabbits and bears crowding around me when he leaned down to kiss me goodnight. Fourth of July again, and the air burns of metal. We are shooting clay pigeons from the dam of our lake. My brother loads the metal arm of the trap. My father stands shotgun butt to the shoulder, eye fielding along the barrel, his thin shadow strung across the barbed wire.

"Pull," he says, and my brother yanks the rope, sends the disk on a long trajectory across the field. The disk flies out like the wizened pigeons of long ago, when they were real and not clay— flying out stunned and unbalanced. My father turns, sweeps the barrel of the gun across the sky, squints, squeezes his trigger finger, bang and recoil jerking him back. Sometimes I see the shotgun pellet hung motionless against the blue before the pigeon shatters.

"Here," my father says, thrusting the gun still hot towards me. "You try."

* * *

My mother calls. When I think of my mother in my childhood, I always think of her and the ladies on those Fourth of Julys chit-chatting at picnic tables scattered throughout our yard, their flowered culottes and white bathing caps like a haven I faded into, shaking my head "no" to the gun, my father and brother grinning even now. Yet, my mother kept a .22 next to her bed for decades, ready to shoot, she reminds me, when I tell her I am thinking of buying a gun, whatever or whomever crossed our fences and maneuvered past our Dobermans. She hunted ducks and birds with my father, practiced shooting single shot targets on a daily basis.

"In case of bear or cougar or man," she tells me, "a shotgun is best." Its single shot, she explains, scatters into a rain of pellets that do not require keen aim to the heart or to the head.

I had forgotten the woman she is.

Could I kill a man? My family thinks not. My mother calls me back and chuckles. "I was talking to your brother about the gun," she says. "Methinks you have no business owning one." I can see my brother grinning like an idiot.

★ ★ ★

What am I afraid to admit? That not having a gun, that not being able to protect myself or my daughters, makes me more feminine, more whomever my mother, my brother or I think I am? Have I really bought into some clichéd patriarchal myth of the chivalrous man who will save me and my daughters, but only if I, if we, are unarmed and "maidenly"?

When Achilles spears Penthesilea, the Amazon warrior princess, and pulls the concealing helmet from her fair head, she lay, it is said, like "the breaking dawn . . . lovely in death," each enemy soldier so overcome by her maiden beauty that they hoped their own wives and daughters at home might be as "sweet as she on her death mound." And the now pining, love-sick Achilles, smote by the imagined bridal bower never to be, sends the body of Penthesilea to her native land for proper burial and honor.

Of course, this is the romantic's version of the myth where men are suitably impressed by women capable of cauterizing their own breasts for battle, yet leaving one breast untouched for their unborn. Other versions of the story are slightly darker— Penthesilea, ominously transgressing "the bounds of nature and her sex," must be punished. Now while she lies dead on the battlefield, Achilles does or does not commit a final humiliating act of necrophilia before sending her deflowered body home for burial. Or, still half-alive, Penthesilea does or does not have her eye gouged out by the unimpressed men folk who contemplate throwing her body to the dogs while she still has "feeling" before being dumped into the Scamander River to drown.

What is the moral here?

"All I want is to beat the crap out of you," that same

Magnum-under-the bed boyfriend said one day to me in passing on the quiet streets of Iowa City after our bitter break up,
long before this world's dark litany of Columbine, Virginia
Tech, Amish schoolchildren, old men who chop off the heads
of girls. Son of that quick-tempered deputy, brother to a diag-
nosed schizophrenic, a rumored embezzler—at that moment
my mind did not conjure up his cold bedfellow, the metal "pea"
that bruised me, but it does now.

★ ★ ★

I wander past the long tables of revolvers with rotating cylinders,
of Colt Pythons, and old Blunderbusses, AK 47s, and semiauto-
matic weapons, what Klebold once bought at a gun show just
like this one to use in his Columbine slaughter where my daughters now eat lunch in the atrium raised from the blood he spilled
in that decimated library.

I am following the heels of two enormously large hunters
who unknowingly part the crowd for me, and, I am ashamed
to say, make my 5'10" frame feel small and dainty. We stop at a
table stacked with cartridges and military shells. The seller of
this ammunition wears canvas shorts and a veteran's vest. He
greets us from a motorized wheelchair, his legs metal and plastic,
his "feet" disappearing like two sledgehammers into the same
kind of black leather shoes my father wore and which for this
man will never crease by walking.

My hunters move on. Across the aisle, another man in cam-
ouflage steps forward, stumbles awkwardly against the table,
his left pant leg too short to cover his plastic ankle, dulled and
yellowed as old Tupperware.

I am in the company of old men, old wars, old guns. I remember a man I once saw up in the mountain town of Victor, in a
narrow 1800s brick bar named Sally's where buffalo and elk

heads festooned in Christmas lights lined the walls. The man stumped across the plank floors with a wooden peg leg, and a metal hook for his hand glinted in the street light—blown off too in some war.

★ ★ ★

When I was a young girl, I once stood ten yards from a bull's eye, a short bow in my left hand, my right hand pulling back hard and shaking on the bow string, my fingers laced around the arrow knocking against my ribs. What I was afraid of, I cannot say, but I could not let the arrow go. The men who would sell me their guns tell me that in the mountains there are bear and mountain lion, cougar and bobcat I might very well never see. Or old drifters, I think. And some two thousand years ago, myth or fact, it is said that Amazon mothers cut off the delicate breasts of their adolescent daughters for war, for the ease of a bow, those young hearts, I imagine, battering against the raw air.

When my daughters were eight, I pulled a small trout from a mountain lake. We had miscalculated the amount of freeze-dried food we needed for a night of camping, so I had to kill the fish because Leonard who owned an aquarium could not. I remember its striking slipperiness, its opaque scales sticking to my fingers as the fish dried in the air, the heave of its gills slowing. I picked up a rock. Once, twice, three times, I struck the fish on the side of its head—the rock suddenly light as air in my hands—before the aching, penny-dark pull and push of its fish mouth stopped. My daughters screamed, rushed from my side to sit on top of a rock and sob above their murderous mother and the shifting earth.

"Androktones," the Greek historian, Herodotus, called the Amazon women. "Killers of men."

The old man with no legs asks if he can help me.

"Not yet," I say.

Speaking the Word

What I remember are the wood and metal school desks with their carved hearts. And the white trash river boy humping the air between bells, my schoolmates in the hall parting like some sea between us until there was only this boy, pizza-faced, mocking me, the white tusks of his socks gleaming beneath his brown polyester pants.

I was thirteen. It was the eighth grade. I had been raped. It's a shock to hear that word here, now, isn't it? It's an ugly word, impossible to prettify. You want to rush over it. You want me to get on with the story of "it," but not the "it." A word to silence, isn't it? Not to speak?

And yet now, twice in less than one year, two women I barely know, two young women have come weeping to me, my own words long silenced tearing out of them: *I have been raped.*

What can I tell them? Of the silence? Of the not speaking except in the courthouse, except in the red dress your mother sews for you, weighted with its tiny blue anchors and the white Peter Pan collar like wilted petals at your neck? How nobody speaks to you of it? How cheerleaders will slouch over the glass pencil case in your school lobby in their micro-minis, not speaking to you, but later, years later, you'll learn, speaking to everyone else: "Why would anybody want to rape her?"

Do you see, how even now, this many years past, I cannot even say it was me?

Of the silence, these women already know: *My mother will not speak of it. My teacher says I should not write of it.* I remember in graduate school, after a decade of poems, of other words only I knew the meaning of—*iron weed* and *gravestone, dead leaves*— when I could finally write down this word, black and unfettered, this man, my teacher, said to me: "I understand what you are saying. Kick it in the teeth and don't ever say it again."

Later, I wrote a story about it. I lied. I said there was a barn and gold hay. I said there was a cemetery caretaker singing drunk in a grave. I said *the earth spewed.* I said *harsh rain, kerosene glow.* And then his son unscrewed a golden urn from the ground, that black ashy oil in the truck's light pouring over his hands, over me—as if this attempt at beauty could be resurrection.

I think I cried like these young women. I think someone comforted me, but all I can remember is the not speaking, the waking and the sleeping and the not speaking, the lying down on my bed and then the waking and the not speaking.

My mother stands in the doorway. The hall light shines through her thin gown, her legs like black triangles, and her dark sex I cannot look at. She is crying.

"I promise," she says. "I promise when you love it will not hurt."

And then, later, when it is time for me to be better, she stands in the same doorway:

"Don't be like other women. Don't let this cripple you."

And we did not speak of it again.

What can I tell her? Of my determined "virginity"? Of how I once stood in a college dorm sick with fear, the phone dead in my hand, still hearing a man's voice I did not know asking if this were me, as if this could be "him"? Or how I gave myself to a frat boy who called himself "poet" simply because I was sick of being afraid? Or how, when they pulled my two daughters from my body, conceived with my true and good husband, in a glorious, unforeseen, loved moment, I thought, *What have I done?*

So many lifetimes ago. There is so little to remember of it.

Perhaps these are the words I should speak:

It was winter. There were dead leaves. His face was snow. And then I bit his finger and he cried.

"Look," he said to me. "Look how you have hurt me."

Spores

Early spring beneath Nipple Mountain and I am thinking about spores, about the mushrooms that every fall billow up out of the earth, silent funnels from some depth we cannot touch, that neither bloom nor flower but in white stillness, filled with billions of dark spores, wait for the crushing foot, the falling branch.

This past semester at the community college, one woman after another in my writing classes wrote of cutting herself, of the primitive carvings she etched into the secret places of her body, of holding the razor blade or a cadre of pills and touching the hot full bath and thinking, *I'll die.*

Camus said, "There is but one truly serious philosophical problem, and that is suicide." Here is the modern ache of chaos and chance, meaninglessness and despair, the absurdities of life Camus exhorts us to embrace. In *The Slender Thread*, Diane Ackerman contemplates the suicide's moment of inevitability— suicide "in a world without God," Camus said—flesh, as I think it, inexorably passing into spirit, vacuity. I think of the woman Ackerman describes, the woman who dies unspeakably in the zoo's lion exhibit, who woke then drove miles at dawn to kill herself, to straddle the morning cool metal, the fence's phallic spikes rigid against her yielding thighs until she crossed over. When was the gravitational shift? When the weight's easy

pull down into the abrupt crevasse men blasted to thwart segue
into the lion's maw, into the pierced jugular, the skull bite, death
anything but instantaneous then, the lions delicately mouthing
her hands first?

I am trying to understand loneliness, my students' and their
desire to hurt themselves, and this woman, her body not even
dust, but dimensionless quantity, spores of what order, of what
magnitude, bridging the sun and world end by end. How does
one reconcile, in the natural world, science and faith? What
words can I give these young women and the women to come
who will weep to me, who will carve their words into paper as
if it were flesh I will hold some late night to read? To grade?

I've read of a fungi that accepts the wound of a tree, fastens
itself where the universe in some roughness—wind, lightning,
the velvet clad antler of an elk—has split the skin, split the tree
into some dark weeping inconsequential to the buried landscape of roots, attaching itself, succor, to that weeping, patient
there until years, years the hard knot of it binds the weeping
wound. In evening when the air and the light fade to their color,
you might stumble upon it, touch its hard shell, say *wing* or *ear*,
breathe in its tiny pepper of spore, and believe, when you turn
away, it gone, as if your struck heart were not already implanted.

Perhaps I should name these mushrooms into beauty for them:
milky caps, shaggy manes, panthers, grisettes, soft knuckles burrowing
out of cow pies, out of elk droppings, a single stalk, or none, lifting them veiled, hooded, puffed out of the subterranean decay.
Wounded ground, stilled spring, I will say, then touch again this old
puff of mushroom, this *calvatia booniana, tete de mort,* autumnal
skull beneath my finger that I once unfurled the spores from.
How hard I know now the flower-sown air, how hard the being
or the not being, the sense and the senselessness, world without God and only the blind self, (but still the self, I'll tell them),
to name it *thou   thee.*

We see only the simple motion of descent...
and ourselves remain imperceptible

—Galileo

Stranded at Mile Marker 72

And where are you?

Mile Marker 72, I say to the CarForRent Extension 4 Emergency Services agent out of Cleveland, you see, I misread the gas gauge, so my acceleration stuttered, slowed, the speedometer plunging 70, 60, 50, the low fuel warning invisible until now, flashing blue, erratic as the robot flailing its metal hooks in warning from my childhood — *Danger, Will Robinson! Danger!* — this rental nosing into the shoulder of the highway and dying, the August sun and humidity so quickly bearing down through the windshield, I get out, despite this rush hour cacophony, this Ohio air so thick and wavy that the soybean crops following me all afternoon distort beyond this highway's utilitarian fence line

And where are you? Kings Mills? Exit 58?

and I say, *no, Mile Marker 72, 72 miles north of Cincinnati*, and it's not the dog days of summer, but the 856 feet in altitude here, that 4,424 foot change from Denver leaving me sodden and weepy all over again, faint against this almost sea-level gravity I am remembering too well from my childhood farm in Murdoch, Ohio, home to weekly summer ice cream socials at the Presbyterian church and the rusted prohibition stills of Grog Run Road, the farmers dead now, my father dead now, twelve years buried in the lost maple grove where pioneers said to their God their first words

And where are you?

Mile Marker 72, I say, this Interstate of my Ohioan childhood, birth place of those who birthed me, grave of my father, where the horses of poets still bend shyly and the wrist of a girl I am stepping gingerly through is the tissue color of this summer sky, blue-wreathed in hints of rain, gingerly, I say, through the weeds of this highway ditch, clutching at my cell phone's umbilical of electromagnetic energy to the human world I have lost, the pink and blowsy shirt my twenty-something daughters sneered at like over-ripened hibiscus too old for either gallant or predatory truck driver to yank his chain, blast the fog horn of his semi, stop for even a mortal second

South of Cleveland

kindly, where the palpable stealth of some hermit crab essay is already backing its shy crustacean body into the hollow shell of this moment, the soybean fields beyond this wire fence gathering over the skeletal stalks of last year's corn crop rotation, Eliot's mermaids singing into the delicate hammer and anvil of my ear, crab scuttling sideways, one-clawed at the bottom of this oceanic humidity, daring to touch what

And what state are you calling from?

in my fifty-first year and I say *Mile Marker 72, Emergency Assistance,* already hunkering down into the ditch of my childhood, my mother telling me, *twenty-five years, the guy who gave you all that trouble, served twenty-five years, his full sentence, released to god knows where,* and *I am finished,* I say, my broken shards—green glass of William Carlos Williams between the walls—only this plastic Seven-Up bottle flattened at the highway's shoulder like road kill, no contagion hospital here but the pesticide drift of a buzzing yellow crop duster, weeds I am slowly dissembling into, wild carrot, gray cone flower, musk thistle, the three leafed ivy I remember from childhood all ruby red and

It's 72 miles north of Cincinnati and we'll not drive out to pick you up

poison in Ohio at Mile Marker 72 where periodic deer strewn along this highway bloat blowsy with may fly and the ants live vertical lives amongst Queen Anne's lace and the milkweed seeds of the newly hatched milk pods I blew as a girl into the evening's blue horizons crumple between the rough tongues of this grass, drone of insects and I am hearing the voices of Persephone's dead and the butterflies

Are you safe? Are you away from the highway? Have you called 911?

flutter at the towering thistle tonguing their white beads dangerously close to the highway's edge, the ants traversing the arch of my bare foot, a sweat bee, ominous, hovering, pumping its stinger up and down above the salt of my skin—I swear I will not look back into the burning sulfur like some wife of Lot—U-Haul,

Zion Christian Assembly driving past as the weeds subsume me,
a gnat finding my ear, blue bottle buzz between the light—and
I begin to smell my stink in this ditch, and the butterflies loop
downwind of me and now a car on this Phlegethon highway
passes by, boiled soul or the gaping maws of the nine-headed
hydra hanging from the windows meaning me

Are you in a safe place?

harm and a strangely red and translucent spider traverses my
foot in the boiling humidity. A gnat on my writing finger lands,
trembles, an ant cleaning its antennas on my foot and I let it,
above me floating buzzard, I hope chicken hawk, more cars with
headlights on, unilluminating, funereal, no network coverage
two hours in and I remember the endless shows my husband
watches of animals eating man, always bear in the background,
or survivor wringing piss from some elephant turd. Don't panic,
they always say, my foot naked, burning, bared to highway salt,
the crop plane's mercurial dust, even the heads of seed flotsam
and light

I'm sorry I can't help you; I'm the reservation desk

and if I sit how long before I become the ditch, the insect-ridden
soybean beyond the iron highway fence, while I said, "finish,"
the car nosing already then into the ditch at the side of the interstate and what you said *twenty-five years*, and I realize nothing has
changed what I said to keep silent ever after rising now from your
lips, your want, not mine, and so I stand up push my sandaled
toes between the wires of fence, heave my leg over the fence post,
it wavering beneath my weight, this weight beneath the skin of
soybeans, the dusty bones of corn stalks and I am remembering

the snakes of my childhood: copperhead, black snake lingering in the corn fields and like a blind woman I tap between the rows with a cane of cornstalk, helpless on the highway, road to childhood, hiking the overpass to stand above the flow of traffic, to wave my phone in the air to catch some power, some

And where are you?

signal, and then the tow truck, lights blinking, and I hazard down the upslope, the soybean and its predators, waving my magic dowser, wand of my cornstalk flailing the sleeping copperhead away, and wobble over the fence into the dry Ohio ditch to the blinking surprise of this man, a farmer, a volunteer fireman, his hands freckled like my father's, liver-spotted, the fine pale hair on his arms speckled with soil, with whatever plant he has just threshed and mown, such intimacy of human hands and arms, the black grime of the thumbnail, cuts of the knuckles,

Are you safe now?

and him following me to a gas station, county road all dusted, his hand in goodbye clapping down on the car frame dark as the blackberries hanging hidden on the other side of this childhood I am remembering, my father's hands thick with their shroud, this farmer patting the open window frame, grinning toothless at me, "Gas caps on the left, darlin'."

I add the *darlin'.*

Winter Garden

I wanted to write of dark earth singing, of spring's ease and soft mouth flower, of birds in light step. But sometimes it is not spring we need, but winter, how it calls us from the walnut dark of our room to kneel in our unplowed gardens, carrying our stick leaf, our musk thistle, our houndstongue.

When my father died, it was not yet winter's solstice, the sun trembling at the brink of the southern sky.

"What do you believe in?" my husband asked me. And I thought of the white river of the Milky Way and the bitter coins of the dark river everlasting beneath the tongues of the dead, and the tears of Myrrha turned to a tree and weeping the holy resin. My father gone, I did not know what I believed, seeing only the snow pieced over the skeletons of my garden.

What my family lived on always was the edge of belief. Somewhere in my mother's past were litany and incense, holy water, and the body of Christ resting on the tongue. But if I think of her in prayer, it is of her alone, in the blue light of evening, in the darkening woods, birds around her singing while she weeps or is glad.

My father's family knew the healing power of the woods and

nature. My father's grandfather, a homeopathic doctor, gathered from the fields and woods the herbs that would heal by inducing the symptomatic dance of disease. But because my father was a doctor of this modern world, I grew up surrounded by white lab coats and black medical bags—science filling the cabinet above our refrigerator with sterilized medicines encapsulated in plastic and white cardboard. That any of these might come from what my great grandfather picked by hand, I never imagined. If there was healing, it was far removed from anything of earth or heaven—prairie willow or yarrow or the blessed hand of the healer pressed against the beleaguered soul. It was a world of reason, of the rational, of man hoisted above the green world by a chain of angels he could never quite touch.

Our ancestors believed that the very gods who smote them down or clutched them to their feathered glory lived in the bodies of plants this season of winter takes and sows forever, again. Yes, there has been a tearing apart from that time, a tearing of heaven from earth, of what is holy from what is concrete, of what is the god's body from the stamen of the plant. But as I stood at my father's side and watched him die while doctors rattled off a catechism of pills and treatments like ancient Egyptians singing the will of gods, I thought, what can we say really but the old words disguised, holding our staffs of snakes like promises of renewal as the bitter skin of the world peels away?

I said we lived on the edge of belief. I now understand my love for the fields and woods, for the green plants in the light evening. I understand now my father refusing his last days, and long before his last days, to take the offerings of his fellow doctors. When I was a child, he would come home from the office, still wearing his white lab coat, and go out to plow the dark silent earth for seed, chaff of the holy clinging to him. I thought then it was what he did to forget the sick and the broken, dust returning to dust. But now I think he was moving through the gods, through the goldenrod and the milkweed, saying his prayers, his incantations to heal whatever body he had touched that day. I hang the roses of his grave like herbs from my kitchen ceiling, watch them stiffen into something I might crumble, take into my body, turn west to east inside me.

What is grief? Is it winter's domain? I stand in my winter garden, what I let stand all winter like the Indians who do not shear the earth at the end of a season of giving, but let everything bend and go under where it stands. All around me, the dead beneath the snow quiver—dried moons of silver, nickels of the heart's wing. What can I take from this garden? What can I rub into my skin, boil down into tea, sprinkle into food?

My daughter stands beside me. My husband has taught her the ways of the Jews, and I am sorry for her that I have not sat *shiva*, covered mirrors, done the edges of ritual that might save us.

Already my daughter forgets my father. Already she does not recognize who I was when young, in the same way those plants bent beneath the snow turn what once was into dreams unrecognizable. I want to tell her that my father walks the Milky Way now, what I once showed her spreading through the mountain dark like a living tissue. I want to tell her that someone has weighed his heart and that he is happy.

Around us, luneria and thyme quicken at the root. We stand beneath the new moon past winter solstice. Only snow fills the air with its light.

"Here," I say to my daughter, and hand her a pod, closed as the heart. Inside, it is all damp spider skein and cusp of seed, what the air cannot yet hold.

"What is heaven?" she asks me. And beneath their stones, the long dead, and the newly, gather, listen.

Adaptations of an Avian Migration Glossary

Circannual rhythm *n*: an internal clock that governs a bird's
yearly life cycle, triggering migration.

Outside my cabin window, a mountain bluebird flutters then alights on an aspen branch still stark with winter. When I was a young girl, I watched my mother feed the wild birds through the long Ohio winters, cardinals, blue jays, towhees wheeling over her as she set the birdfeeder on the ground, filled it with sunflower seed and millet, her breath hanging in the air against our thorned Russian Olives. She named the birds one by one from the sky.

Ten years after my father's death, forty years after I watched her feed the wild birds, my mother is going blind. *Glaucoma. Macular degeneration.* The world in front of her slowly obscures. Grayness, like a glacier, calves, floats freely in front of her. Anything she sees telescopes down to a miniature of itself, every week a specialist pricking her ulcerated eyes with a needle to stem the bleeding behind them.

The bluebird eyes me through the window glass, watches the nest cradled on the porch's timber beam. A thousand aspen trees offer the gaping notches of their broken limbs, but this bluebird wants last year's nest, wants the old scent of its young, the impressions of their slight bodies I imagine intact—genetic landmarks that this bluebird has tracked down, wise, I think, to the ways of its off-springs, to what scientists call "spring over-shoot," when birds fly past their normal breeding grounds, this mother bird in the failing light alone.

"I hope," my mother tells me, "I stroke out before I go blind."

Fall *v*: when weather forces large numbers of migratory birds off course and they come to rest somewhere they do not normally occur.

It is fall. It is raining and you are weeping unknown to your father by the pond where you have brought him. Shadow, leaf, branch—all this, you think, is your father.

This evening, I hear a soft persistent thud against the cabin window. The mother bluebird, blue-tipped, dull with her gender or age, poises on the deck post and then launches herself again and again at the nether world of my window—last daylight, the brooding pines, the skeletal aspen and my face at the heart of it all. Some days, I find two or three birds fallen to the ground, stunned by that hardness and their longing.

Flyaway *n*: a route many migrating birds of various species use while migrating.

He forgets my mother first. "Who are you?" he asks. "Where is the other lady who takes care of me?"

The nurses call this "sundowning." As his light diminishes,

shadows lengthen and my father's suspicions of my mother change to terror. He runs out of the house into that final September evening and hammers on the neighbor's garage door.

"Help me," he calls out. "I've been kidnapped."

The police subdue him with a straight jacket.

I travel in early October to visit him in the state psychiatric unit.

"They can't find the right medication for him," mother warns me. "He seems overly sensitive." We find him in a wheelchair, in a small TV room. He is dressed in a patient's backless hospital gown, slumped over the metal tray used to wedge him in, his glasses sliding sideways off his face.

I am weeping. "Look," my mother says to him. "Look what I have brought you."

He smiles, grasps my hand, and pulls it toward his face.

"Watch out," my mother says as he slowly bends my fingers back.

Great Circle routes *n*: flight paths that represent the shortest distance between two points on the globe.

Do you see how it is still not now? Not this "now" that has no father in it, but the now when your mother could bring him to you, and the past, too, like she always does every time you think of her, this past of rain you are remembering this very moment—your father's grave fresh with flowers, and the dead grass beside it white with the chalk marks for where your mother would be laid. Do you understand this—standing in the grave of your mother, the soles of your shoes slick with the mud of your father's?

My sister and I wait in the graveyard that fronts my father's farm. Already we are sisters again, my father, this king of rain, not yet dead, but dying. We bend through the wild honeysuckle together, fallen gravestones, "My Beloved," all around us, whole families lying at our feet.

It is getting darker. An orange moon swells over the tree line,

and we can barely trace the carved names around us. My mother
drives my father back to join us. She parks near the fence along
the graveyard lane and gets out.

"This is where we'll be," my mother says, and paces off the
lengths of coffins.

You have no words for this, only bird, only air, tender hand that sings.

Leading Lines *n*: physical features of the earth . . . that large
numbers of birds must pass through or stop at.

You are walking with your father past the vast geographies of childhood.
Here is the pond and its secret spring. Here, the pale carp spilling past
the dam into the field below. Here, the fence line your mother and father
strung through the long heat, the sounds of their voices you hear even
now as if through a girlhood window.

My mother calls me with yet another story of yet another
eighty-year-old friend going to live with her daughter or debat-
ing going-to-live-with-her-daughter.

"I think that's good," she tells me. "I think she'll be happy." And
then she chuckles, as she always does, no matter what my reply.

I see it all now as a great migration: all the fathers and husbands
dead, and the white-haired women, whom my mother half-blind
still drives to shopping and dining, drawn by the sudden cold—by
the bones suddenly too frail, the winter suddenly too fast at the
leaking window—to the homes of their children. Scientists call it
"leap frog migration" for what the birds do, unexpectedly, out of
necessity, a winter breaking harsh and unforgettably, triggering
the happily nested into an increase of fat, a hormonal longing that
stirs even the caged to follow the long migratory arc of a star, a
magnetic field made visible, the bodies of our children, I understand now, the far land we fly to.

Magnetic compass *n*: the mechanism that allows a bird to nav-
igate by locating magnetic north.

My mother has fallen into a geranium bed. She has stepped out
of the half-light of my sister's SUV into the day's blindness and
stumbled. I have flown to meet her in Kansas City with my sister
because mother has said to me the word *despair*. The year after
my father died, my mother began to fall. Walking out of restau-
rants into the early evenings, as if the whole sidewalk cracked
open, she would fall, her hands and arms clenched to her chest,
one wild howl, and no move to catch herself.

She tells us the story of going to see the first eye doctor with
my father and discovering that she had low-pressure glaucoma
and would one day go blind. My father, the physician, already
sinking into the oblivion of Alzheimer's, trimmed his fingernails
throughout the doctor's verdict without a word.

"Do you remember," my mother asks us, "when that pile-
ated woodpecker hammered through our new porch screens?"

And I think of my father, wordless before my mother's great
grief, how once he waved that bird's blind terror back through
the torn rents.

Migration *n*: the seasonal movement of birds in response to
change in food availability, habitat or weather.

---

*You enter the apse of trees. You walk beneath the willed cathedral of
branches, the moon a bent rod. Always there is this aftermath, this lev-
eled snow over the small temples of the earth.*

In December of 1998, in Ohio, in the locked facility of a small
rest home, after spending three months in a state psychiatric
ward where he was overdosed and over-restrained, my father,
a family doctor for some thirty-five years, died at the age of

seventy. What he died of my family does not readily speak of: the tangled plaque of Alzheimer's that knots the brain, TIAs— Transient Ischemic Attacks, tiny strokes, brief, but capable of brain cell death. My mother, his living guardian, would not let the surgeons insert the tube he had once said he did not want into his stomach when he stopped eating.

"I think," mother says, "that he just gave up. That he decided this is the way he would go."

Nocturnal Migration *n*: migration during the hours of darkness.

Tonight, the moonlight falls like snow into the field hollows. My dog and I walk up the two-wheel lane from the cabin, the sun gone blind behind Little Bull Mountain. An owl calls softly to its mate, arcs over me, disappears into the darkness. I stand quietly in the old snow, listening, the night heavy around me, above me, a few stars, the white face of the moon.

Your father has found the shell of a turtle, more bone than shell. It is summer and you carry it for him to the tool shed's window to dry, to show it to your mother. Like delicate lace—the sun lighting it and the bones ossifying in air, and your mother and father and you, for a moment, glad. And all through the long new winters, you think—lost and losing and yet to lose—how you will think of it (as if I could) beautiful beneath the rain, beneath the silent scapulars of snow.

Staging Post *n:* stopovers where large numbers of migratory birds traditionally pause to feed before moving on.

Your brother is weeping. Your sister strokes your father's arm. We are here, father. It is raining, she says, and we are here, and you bend down to touch his cool dark mouth with its far wishing moon.

A few years ago, I looked up "dying by starvation." *Changes in*

*blood chemistry, loss of bone density, cardiac arrhythmia, severe muscle
loss, renal, liver and pancreatic impairment*—endless, the list of loss.
But ten years ago, twelve hundred miles away from my father, I
did not even think of this as he lay dying, my mother saying to me
over the phone, "He is going now. He has stopped eating. This is
what he wants." Even as my family stood together at last in the
long linoleum light of the nursing home, my sister and I flying
in for that last miraculous five minutes of his fated life, watching our father in his railed bed as he once watched his mother,
his whole body buckling in the faint air, I did not think of this.

Vagrancy *n:* a biological phenomenon when animals, including
migrating birds, lose their way.

---

*Rain coming down and the birds singing in rain. It is summer, and
you are walking with your father past the woods he planted, what
he cannot remember. Where the trees bend to the pond, he is a pale
specter echoed in water and you hold his hand as you have held your
daughters' hands.*

The first moment I recognized my father's confusion, my
sister and I had flown in from the West to surprise him for his
retirement party. He stood before us in the soft Ohio river rain
at a broken farm gate he could no longer fix, already half-fa-
ther then, already the white mist in the dark places of the trees
above him torn like some ragged childhood sky as he peered at
us—strangers.

What he died of was not a sudden onslaught at first, but a
slow wasting away, a genetic predisposition he feared all my conscious life. In the 1960s, he watched his own mother curl into the
fetal oblivion of what he called "true Alzheimer's." In the 1990s,
my mother marked his dresser drawers with pieces of masking
tape—*Pants. Sweatshirts. Socks.* Still we could not name it.

Zugunruche *n*: a restlessness observed in birds as the time to migrate approaches.

My mother and I sit in the half-dark of her den, a shrine she has left to my father. I have come to visit her in Ohio and we have spent the day wandering through her house, writing down the names of things she wants me to want when she is gone. From the picture frame above the desk, my father smiles, holds out his prized fish to us. I want to ask my mother how she did it, how she let my father, no matter what he may have wanted, go the way he did.

She asks me to download a form from the Internet.

"I don't know how," she tells me. "You have to help me."

DNR, the file reads. I look at my mother.

"Do Not Resuscitate," she says.

Wind and Fire

June, and the wind-borne smoke of the Wallow and Horseshoe
Two wild fires in Arizona and New Mexico ride day after day the
southwestern wind up the Arkansas Valley until my eyes burn.
Wind is the mitigating presence here, the reaper, I've called it,
peeling back the pinned leaf until air whitens the aspens to bone,
to the coral of bone. Fire season, and already I am regretting
the given: this droughty June field lithe with its singular grasses,
its buried names, the hard clavicles of its vanished longhorns.

This afternoon, the sun settled on the snuffed out mountains
of Little Bull and Pisgah like a chip of quartz the old prospectors
followed into mother lodes of granite and gold. This landscape
wants the pastoral, I think, the single swallow flicking to earth,
end-stopped and punctual as absence. But for too long now, I
have heard nothing of the world but this man hurting this man,
hurting this woman, this child, and now, all day fire, and I am
wondering the small ways of mercy, of my own, wondering
when *eleos,* mercy, will pour down like an oil from heaven, *Lord
have mercy, Lord have mercy,* said a hundred times in some liturgy
I don't yet know the name of. Here, are the words of wind: *wind
blown, wind borne, wind break, wind broken.* Do you see how the
pattern emerges? *Wind flaw, wind gap,* and now the *winding sheet*

for the corpse and the *windlestraw* we bury it beneath.

Once the wind was your mother, we said, as if we had burned her clean in our mourning the day we buried her in her pine box and your family came to our home to sit *shiva* and I did everything wrong. And then the ash from the Hayman Fire, started by some forest ranger, a crazed woman burning bitter letters of love in a circle of stones, she claimed, fell from the sky as if nothing we grieved that day had color but what we could give it, the wind, your mother, we said, like an ark returning to us from a far sea, black with its carbons and little dusks of blue.

Drought-induced, wind-driven miles from here, those fires smolder unchecked through empty arroyos and dried scrub, their smoke closing down highways and ushering whole cities into their homes. I had never known to fear fire. Never known it wild, wind-borne. In the sixties, in the wet Ohio country I grew up in, long before acid rain, the ozone's gape or the glaciers' great melt, my cul-de-sac neighbors blazed their autumnal leaves with a single match, everywhere plumes of smoke rising as if watch fires burned from our small suburban yards. I remember the embers, flung skyward, how they floated above us like paper lanterns released to appease gods we didn't know or need, each burning shred as red to me now as the gills of the fish I told you we sometimes pulled from our deep-barreled creeks and let gape in the sodden summer air until eternity, all this the sanctuary of mercy we laid our hearts in.

I tell you there is a geography to wind, and it is a geography of family, our families, a sightless boundary between whole continents, wind our only constant here beneath this Nipple Mountain, whole canyons of air pushing down from the jet stream, then upslope to the free range cows that graze in their slow diurnal orbits.

I think of the sailors of long ago who sailed like me across the blank infinities of their maps into unknown worlds strewn with their dragons. Of those, becalmed, desperate at the stilled equator, at the windless latitudes of whole new worlds, throwing overboard what could be sacrificed.

Mercy, they said, whole seas filled with the bodies of their horses. *Mercy.*

Eyes like almonds and skin darker than most, our daughter once wrote. *Even in the harsh pale of winter, I am a girl not unfamiliar to ethnic jokes, confusion, and even cruel insults.*

I think of your mother—did I love her enough?—a girl once fleeing across the steppes of Russia to escape the fires of the pogrom. And of the Hebrew word, *rachamim*, from the Old Testament, the second most used word for God's mercy, *rechem* its root—*mother's womb, love that springs from pity.*

"My mother bit my toes to keep them from freezing," your mother would tell us, this wizened little woman in a blue bathrobe and tiny slippers lifting her toes off the carpet so her son, you, could run a sweeper beneath her chair. She walked through frozen tundra, rowed across the blackest rivers of family lore in the boats of gypsies and thieves, sailed here to a Wyoming homesteading father she hadn't seen in ten years.

"I couldn't speak to him," she said.

"My mother always loved my sister best, the pretty one," she would tell us in her house, green with her plants and the roots of plants she nursed in tiny bottle caps and fragile teacups. I remember seeing her through the window of my hospital door the day our daughters were born. Just cut, drugged with morphine, I said, "Don't let her in," to the nurse. "Don't let her in." Later I watched her lift our premature daughters from their incubators,

kiss the red stork bites spread like a whole country at the back of
their necks, the blue Mongolian stains on their fleshless rumps.

Fire watch begins before the last months of winter here. Men
ski and snowshoe into the deepest drifts of places we call *Wild
Basin, Grizzly Peak, Deadman Hill* to measure snowpack with their
metal tubes, always the snow found wanting, and so dread takes
hold. All day the firemen have done what they call "anchor and
flank the fire." You see, I am learning the terms of fire. *Candling*
and this means a single tree burns from its roots. Say *fingers of
fire*, and these are the spot fires of flying embers. Let fire move
into wind, and it's a *backing fire*. Let it burn beneath the surface
and its *understory*.

Our daughters are Jewish or they are not Jewish. They are German
or they are not German. English or not English. Dutch or not
Dutch. Russian. Polish. I remember the Orthodox Jews when
we were first married, strolling past our house on High Holy
Days, the women, who wore *sheitels*, wigs, to cover their hair on
Sabbath, silently watching me roll my double-stroller to West
Colfax and across to Sloan's Lake. No, they would have said,
not Jewish, had they spoken to me. And of our neighbor, Mrs.
Schneider, polishing her worn linoleum kitchen until it shone,
her couch and chairs encased in clear plastic, the first survivor
of a Holocaust camp I knew, "thief of rotten German potatoes,"
she called herself, a woman I am ashamed to say I barely liked,
her husband-to-be, those many years ago when she was young,
broadcasting the names of his family to the air, this neighbor boy
she knew when she stood at the train station hearing his voice,
the war as if ended, and passing through the crowd to perhaps
touch him, to marry him, how she would tell me, too, if I asked
her, "No."

You said the smell was the Hayman fire on the day your mother died. Three in the morning, unable to sleep, I sit on our balcony to watch the small universe of our spotting scope. They say the wind affects the earth's rotation. They say the wind can feel the earth *turn underneath it* as I do now. Above the mountain ridge, along the pine, a new curtain of fire burns some fifty miles away across summits called Poverty Mountain and I am seeing fire as I have never seen it before, its flare and smolder, its small jump flames that blossom, extinguish.

They say in ancient Athens that only the wretched could know the altar of Eleos, goddess of mercy and pity, make it sacred with what they cast off: tears, their hair shorn in grief hanging. This should be about your mother now, but this man, Mrs. Schneider's husband, long dead, keeps walking into this—his black overcoat and fedora, his pipe of ash and ember. I stand behind the lilac bushes on Winona Court, in West Denver again, holding the garden hose to water lilacs. I cannot stop crying. The Orthodox Jews are walking the streets for Sabbath and I am crying because someone has told me I may never have children. Then I smell the burning, and Mr. Schneider stands near me on the other side of the lilacs, this neighbor who once stood at a train station at the end of a war, calling out the names of his family one by one—father, mother, brother, sister, uncle, aunt, cousin, nephew, niece—all dead, Mrs. Schneider told me. All dead.

"What's wrong?" he asks. And I can barely answer him for shame.

"You'll be okay," he says. "Okay." And I watch his pipe smoke settle in the lilacs between us.

Look how I could almost end this—*eleos,* mercy, circling back. And now *olos kaustos*: burnt sacrifice—

But do you remember this? Our daughters, five, and you wanting to read to them *Anne Frank* and *The Devil's Arithmetic,* so that they could know better their heritage, know the yellow star, the ghetto, the Jewish girl transported back to the concentration camps, back to the ovens, the black spew. The fire.

And how I begged you, no.

Talismans of the Whirlpool

Their father floats his six-foot telescope between binary stars—talismans of the Whirlpool Galaxy. Twenty-four years, the whole of our marriage, longer than our daughters' eighteen years, he has searched the darkest skies, searched for that smudge of spiral arm and star cluster, of dust cloud, and the black hole at this galaxy's heart.

We are alone. Again.

This morning, the woman who owns *Splendid Treasures*, the antique shop in the ruins of an old mining town three miles up Phantom Canyon from here, calls us "empty nesters" and raises her arms in triumph.

"You did it," she says, amidst the detritus of fallen households.

Once, on an August night late as this, as their father scanned the universe, I kissed our tiny daughters who were sleeping beneath a whole shower of stars and felt the earth, beneath this radiant point, turn. Tonight, our daughters sleep elsewhere beneath these quiet stars, and their father, standing beside me, is all shadow, my own "dark matter" against the soft egg of the moon.

I watch the vague shapes of constellations, which I still have no names for, encircle us. Our daughters fall away, and I can only measure their leaving now the way Galileo once measured distance and time: with the breadth of these hands, with the falling of this late summer seed, with the silences we count between the murmurings of the paired owls we love—lonely pulse of our hearts tapping unbidden, uncounted at our wrists.

I think of Galileo, tipping his primitive telescope to the once unknowable sky and finding for the first time the craters of a moon and then fixing forever the *Inquisitor's* terrible sun into the center of our Copernican galaxy. *Spira Mirabilis—Wonderful Spiral*—the astronomers call the Whirlpool we search for. *Mira*, Hebrew for *oh wondrous one*—what we named our daughter who came after, crying into this world when her twin was taken from my body so quickly, so silently, with such little breath that I could not see her as apart from me for a whole day, a whole night fevered from that birthing until I wheeled myself in to watch her sleeping in her glass incubator, her sister beside her, the still centers of my life, there.

In their father's astronomy book, the Hubble telescope magnifies the Whirlpool galaxy into a glory of such heat and light, reflecting far beyond what the primitive glass of Galileo's lens or the mirrors of this hand-built telescope, which their father keeps sweeping against our darkest skies, could possibly hold. *Spira Mirabilis* is the mathematician's dream, the precise symmetry of an infinite curve repeated over and over again on this earth, in these heavens—in the Whirlpool's spiraling arms, in the hurricane's vortex, the clustered seeds of a sunflower.

"The hand of God," Galileo said—measurable, manifest in this spiral nebula that my daughters' earth-bound father wants to capture, to hold for a brief moment in the telescope's eye piece, in the cold curve of his palm that has held me, too.

"Celestial womb," I tell him, star birth and blue stars curving geometrically, perfectly from that galaxy's holed center through the strings of space and time, the light years yet to touch us, to touch those whom I can no longer keep close.

I remember my daughters inside me. My wanting body so long arid that their father and I could not believe their quickening, the tiny salt springs of them erupting from within my sad bones into such small creatures—such small moons—form and form-lessness shadowed in the ultrasound beneath their placental bubbles. Month after month, we watched the curve of their waxing bodies, those particulates of stars, galaxies of our own making, folding in and out like some earthly night blooming flower that opens and closes before the first light. Even now I remember the masked surgeon cocking his head to better see that televised Yankee's game, bantering the lore of Koufax and backdoor sliders with their father as he pierced my navel with a needle to withdraw the first shed cells of my daughters.

"It's harder with twins," he said, glancing down at my shiver-ing, blue-veined belly, "not to stick 'em."

Below now, nestled in my pubic hair, is the ragged mid-line incision where a woman surgically cut through my skin, through the uterine wall, into the bag of birth waters—their hearts fal-tering, so each daughter pulled from me with her gloved hand. I remember, years ago, my mother telling me that with her chil-dren's leaving, with my leaving, she had nothing.

Fifty and nothing. My age.

I watch the tiny, erratic satellites that zigzag perpetually over my head and the low moon spinning the constant contrails of night jets into light. Galileo said the universe was written in the language of the mathematician, that without understanding its symbols we are left "wandering in a dark labyrinth." I wonder what we will have now, with their leaving, their father and me.

"You know," their father says, as he calibrates and fiddles with his telescope, the red bulb of his flashlight circling the darkness between us, "these galaxies are spinning further and further apart until finally there will be no stars. Nothing."

Today, my daughter calls me to tell me about a theory she has learned in college, of time eradicated, even the bending light of stars gone into the now and the now, existence—without time—everlasting, our spatial world a collage of what is past and present and future—all fragmented, all parallel, all immortal.

Consoled, I think.

"I don't understand it," my daughter tells me.

I think of Daedalus, father of Icarus who flew too close to the sun and fell to the sea, that craftsman strapping his beloved son with feathers to free him from some human labyrinth and then watched how the boy's arms, passionate as the dawn, floated irretrievably skyward, the feathers he crafted into the measured curve of bird wing, light as air beneath the pitiless sun. How many times did he search the sky for Icarus, call out to his lost child, that moment in this theoretical universe sealed in forever and all the long, lonely years after? Like every crystalline moment of our lives, my daughter's physicist says, fixed forever, every love of ours lost, not lost, lost as we dream again and again of the bobbing sea, the blind ships beneath our emptied skies like driftwood.

My friend, another empty nester, tells me, "I don't know what I grieve for," and I watch the moon throwing its constant flux of shadows on this little world I can name into being: Phantom Canyon, Cripple Creek, Nipple Mountain. Daughters. Father. Husband.

"Immortality is all around us," the physicist says. "Our task is to recognize it."

Like Galileo tonight, their father and I are searching for the waning and waxing of Venus, for the named moons of Jupiter, for what moves us in the far emptiness beyond our human time, our human selves. Somewhere between the measured stars of Cygnus and Draco, of Orion and Serpens lies that God of Galileo, infinite, eternal, mathematic. And somewhere below Alkaid, what their father names for me, end star of the Big Dipper's handle, daughter of the Bear, what I showed our daughters each time we lay down beneath the Milky Way, road of our most ancient gods, lies the Whirlpool Galaxy.

"The gifts of angels," I told our daughters that night when we watched not stars I know now, but the dust of comets a thousand years old that I could fit in my hands, the broken pieces of planets I will never see lighting those dark skies, the warm flesh of my daughters I still press my face against. Soon the constellation Perseus will shower its meteors over us again, where the head of Medusa waits to turn every moment of us into stone.

Their father tells me we are near everything now. Beneath the jets' hum and the light wash of the city, I press my eye to his telescope until it blurs and tears in the cold night air. Here is the dark matter of this world, its smudge of gas and stars, whole galaxies that Galileo never dreamed of, what their father, what I, cannot yet grasp, drifting and everywhere.

Wren

Existence precedes essence. —Jean-Paul Sartre

The wren, a house wren—*troglodytidae,* "cave dweller," *dru-wid-s,* "oak-knower"— chits at its nestlings from the deck rail, moth, caterpillar, grasshopper, slug pinned in its beak. Relentless forager, this common wren is all existence. And my father is all dream and shadow space, essence these past twelve years that enters my sleep, comes to the side of my bed where sometimes in dreams I weep.

"Forty-five hours," he says, "I traveled to come here," as if death were tangible place, afterlife from which my father can periodically visit me, tell me what I cannot hear nor finally remember.

Today is all about the tenuousness of this life: how already I see there is no way to apply real fire prevention rules to this place, that even when a community has spent millions of dollars and hours teaching and helping its residents to create wildfire defensible spaces, the humidity will drop; there will be no rain for a month; dry thunderstorms will whip the wind through the canyons; heat over a hundred degrees will make any spark fire-worthy and the fire will jump ridges, send hot spots miles away, fill the air with ash and ember, burn the crowns of trees and the ladders of vegetation that lead to them. Burn us. We have had two short rain showers: air blessedly cool and then rain for only a few moments, even in that, the tinder grass softened. But it's not enough: the cinquefoil bushes shrivel, the aspens have begun to turn color two months early, the dead grass from last year is the only grass on the ground, nothing green except where a few natural springs rise or gullies in the watershed push rain and snow water into low areas and we see emerald green, astonishing in all the bleached grass. We talk of monsoons: What if they don't come? Why should we believe they will?

I begin to understand more about the existential view of loneliness, what brought Nietzsche to madness, Thoreau to the woods. It is not a loneliness of things, of what is lost and now no longer, my father this time pulling from his neck and my bed small bugs he bursts into droplets of blood, complaining how they plague him, even in my dreams his death made visceral.

It is not that loneliness: it is the *"angoisse* of human freedom that I am alone to be whoever I want to be," Sartre's existence preceding essence, essence what we are, here, now, meaning. Nature teaches me everything. I watch the house wren on her never-ending feeding cycle for her nestlings. I can hear the nestlings in the wren house *churr* in response to the rattling chatter of their returning mother. She announces herself early on the deck railing, then hops to the pine tree, bypassing the crazed aerial displays of the hummingbirds at their feeder. All the time, she chitters, her nestling responding until she hops to the tiny perch at the opening and pokes her head inside, dropping in whatever she has found, dead or living, to her ravenous young, their waiting beaks opening over and over again until she is all existence, their existence.

Leonard says I am the least spiritual person he knows. Is this true? Do I not even believe in spirit, in a place for the soul? He laughs that I want to be cremated: not even a physical body left for the hereafter. *What do you love?* he asks me—*not nature*, he says. But, yes, nature, nature in solitude—what I see of the patterns of existence here and of non-existence, what I can make into metaphors of what is holy out of the viscosity of the physical world. Yes, here the wren is simply bird, not king nor druid seeking knowledge, not shape-shifter. But for two weeks, I have watched it hover at the door of the wren house we tied to a tree, flashed a light into the darkness it feeds, and then seen a swooping stellar jay, omnivorous scold, hook its claws to the front of the wren house, poke its beak through the door, *meat-eating bird,* Leonard tells me, *a robber jay intent on those nestlings.*

Existential loneliness says there is hope for affirmation and creativity outside the mundane world, if you can turn away from it. What do I take away from the jay clasping the wren house to its beating blue breast, the nestlings seconds away from death before I drive the jay out, while the mother wren continues her endless cycle of flight and forage? Or that on the twenty-sixth of each December, after the birth of our Christ, twenty-five days after my father's death, this little wren, this little passerine song bird, symbol of the past year, Celtic legend says, was stoned for centuries on the day of Wrenning? Or that its body was tied to a pole in procession "to mark," as those who killed it said, "its betrayal" of Saint Stephen, protomartyr of Christianity, prototype for the suffering of Christ, man who prayed even for those who stoned him to death?

Druids, name-sakes for our little wren, believed in the soul's immortality. *Existentialists*, Leonard says, *do not believe in an afterlife.*

I go outside into the night air where the waning moon settles itself in the clouds, this high plains meadow so dry the grass looks like snow shadow beneath the rustling trees. I think of fire prevention and realize its hopelessness here, how grass fire burns faster on the upslope, and all upslopes lead to this cabin. The wren house, ransacked I fear, is dark and silent, each of us—wren, nestlings, my father, me lost to our own isolation.

James Longenbach, in *The Resistance to Poetry*, says, "if the word *and* permits us to wander, the word *or* forces us to stagger, doubling backward, falling down."

Is this essence or existence I am living?

*It is impossible that anything should
have by nature the principle of moving in
a straight line; or, in other words, toward a
place where it is impossible to arrive,
there being no finite end*

—Galileo

Aspen

I cut hard with the loppers on the finger-width root sucker just below the thin leaf rot and the subalpine grass that cover the rotting granite. In our little writer's paradise 9,600 feet above the sea, squirreltail, mutton grass, sedge, fescue and nodding brome feather-in our "landscaping" beneath this vast colony of aspen. Our dying aspen. I've lost count of the denuded trees our neighbors kindly chainsaw down for us, of the felled limbs I've sawed into kindling, always it seems the downy woodpecker balancing somewhere above me on the afflicted trunks, harbinger tapping out its Morse code of heart rot and inevitable fall.

Is this SAD, Sudden Aspen Decline, the aspen die-off that has wiped out hundreds of thousands of acres of aspen throughout the West, sparked perhaps by the early 2002 drought with its sparse rainfall and snowpack and decimated reservoirs? Or simply our stupidity, or, worse, our hubris to think we could shoehorn in a little cabin between the silver-barked aspens we love and a few brooding Engelmann Spruce and *not* have an impact?

I stand at a ravine with my arms full of dead wood. It is a deep cut in the earth left long ago by the persistent snowmelt and violent cloudbursts the long-timers still talk of during the halfhearted monsoons of our recent Junes and Julys. We are at the backside of *Tava—Sun Mountain Sitting Big*—what the ancient Ute Indians, *Blue Sky people,* called our "Pikes Peak." They believed the Great Spirit made this shining mountain, once beacon across the eastern plains, pouring snow and ice down out of the sky. I wonder what rain and snowfalls they had those centuries ago, try not to think of climate change and my husband's dire warnings. Here, our altitude is some 4,500 feet below the summit of Pikes Peak and, on a good year, our precipitation averages only sixteen inches. We're ten years into the drought's long-standing wake, the ravine like an inverted monolith now hardened as if the waterless moon cratered here where the dogs and the elk nose for a trickle of spring water and where the stricken aspen crack before the harsh downslope of winter wind. Late May, and our suspect weather station poised on the shed roof records a mere 1.67 inches of moisture. Month? Year?

The Colorado State Forest Service posts a whole list of possible aspen tree diseases: trunk rot, which might be the more poetic "heart rot" I've heard of, sooty bark canker, oystershell scale, ink spot disease, sawflies, and elk scarring, the last most visible on our trees where the wintering elk teethe at the bark to eat the inner pulp. The list is long and insidious, but none of it quite matches the cyclical demise of our aspen: the sudden shriveled leaves in this crown branch and then that branch, the pitchy black yawn at the trunk's base, the holes the birds fill with their nests where the branches have broken. Not even SAD matches the copious shoots, the grossly overgrown stands of saplings the Forest Service calls "dog hair," that have sprouted around our cabin between the dying aspens. Poor wind propagators, aspens respond to imminent death with sucker roots, clones of the dying tree sprouting from root "teats" and ensuring continuance of the colony. Aspen, it is said, is our oldest living fossil. But surely, not these wind-twisted shoots, these sparse leavings?

I debate thinning and clear-cutting, still unsure of my role in these borrowed woods.

I remember the first time we entered this place, momentary guests of an eon in the shadow of a great erosional mountain worn by wind and rain to its granite heart. They say the crowns of aspen allow the beloved dead to be reborn. They say that the trembling leaf beneath the tongue fills the mouth with spirit. And so we lay down beneath the quaking, beneath the *opulus tremul*, trembling poplar, light then dark then sea sound and breath and us naming it all *home home*, already bird song in the woundings.

Naked Seeds

So we fix our eyes not on what is seen, but on what is unseen. For what is seen is temporary.

—*2 Corinthians 4:18*

Drought, again. Smoke from the Springer fire in Elevenmile Canyon sifts over our Nipple Mountain, settles into the Arkansas River Valley some 5,500 feet below us. Second fire of a predicted long and daunting western fire season: the first, lightning-sparked, this second, a rumored potshot into a propane tank near Indian Paint Brush Ranch. Despite the state's red flag warnings. Despite the frizzled gold banner of June or the pine needles' rasp beneath our feet. Only the hardiest plants flower now: stonecrop in the granite crevasses, boulder raspberry near the aspen shoot, the weedy pussytoes prematurely seeding this air white.

I thought not to come here, to this mountain cabin I love. Bitter at the thermal updraft, bitter at the La Nina or the El Nino, at global warming, carbon emissions, fossil fuels. Bitter at the inevitability of my mother's failing eyesight, at whatever burns what is spring and fragile into such white tinder. But, of course, I came, incapable of not—here, the trembling aspen, here, the

granite glory holes, the solitary hawks riding their cusps of wind.
This time, I told myself, in such drought I would know even
the pine cone, seed-carrier of the conifer, touch it as if I could
touch even the yellow tears of the Dryad nymph Pitys turned to
a sacred pine and weeping her resin against the northern wind.

A Buddhist I read said there are six kinds of loneliness, the last
and hardest to bear, though she does not name it, what I might
call Nietzsche's existentialism, to ultimately embrace life, loneliness, moment, self as is— bitter, unbitter. My mother will not
come here this summer. Another eye surgery has left her partially immobile in a world not of darkness, but of granulation
and distortion.

"I fear this will be it," my mother says over the phone. "One
surgery after another until finally there is nothing left."

The wind holds the Springer smoke at bay. After ten years of
intermittent drought, our woods are a mishmash of broken
limbs and dry fuel ready to ignite at any spark. This late summer,
even the aspen turn early, colonies stressed into the pointillism
not of gold, but wan yellow, pale harbingers of some brief and
grievous fall. Pinecones litter the shadows of our Lodgepole
and Douglas fir. Some stay closed to my touch, awaiting some
great ladder of fire to open their wooden scales, light the crowns
of trees, burn down whole stands to ash, to dust. Precursors to
these droughty flowers I mourn, wilting each day around me,
these pine cones are "naked seeds," seed-bearers of the Gym-
nosperm, unenclosed by ovaries. Three hundred and nineteen
million years ago—*what is the temporal*, I ask myself, *what eternity?*— Gymnosperms emerged, fourteen million years before
what the scientists call an "extinction event," the Carbonifer-
ous Rainforest Collapse that separated rainforests into isolated
"islands," crushed vegetation into the coal seams we, ironically,

mine now for the fossil fuels that warm, irrevocably, our air and
oceans. Ritual drought, ritual burning: the scorched earth regen-
erative, fertile for the seed so naked before the willful world.

Last summer, midnight, no moon, I took my mother outside to
stand in the thin air beneath rivers of stars, of constellations of
gods and bears, of flare stars and red giants.

"See?" I asked her, but she could not.

Emerson once said, "Man is a god in ruins," and I think of
my mother "readying her affairs" with the lists she mails telling
us what we may and may not do: *No obituary. No memorial. No
wake. Only ashes.*

"Funerals are for the living," my sister tells her.

"What," my husband asks me, "is behind this?" And I remember, many years ago, birdsong in the Midwestern woods my
mother walked, chaff of seed in her sweat, fields she worked,
gardens she tilled, her hands flush with raspberries wide as the
coins once placed on the eyes of the dead.

"See?" she would say. "See?"

I read that the Pope bears a pine cone on his staff, seed of the
evergreen, something holy, I think, though my mother would
not care if I told this to her. And that the wooden petals of the
pine cone, like leaves patterned on a flowering stem or the seeds
fixed in the wandering eye of a sunflower, spiral into Fibonnaci
numbers, nature's mathematical order that exists everywhere.
And attached to the third ventricle of our cerebrums is a tiny
pine cone-shaped gland, the pineal body, which regulates our
circadian rhythms, sensing light and its absence, the body pre-
pared for sleep or wakefulness.

Descartes believed the pineal gland held the soul, migratory
threshold of self and spirit. The ancients and the occultists called

it the "third eye," eye of the Cyclopes, blacksmiths to the gods, makers of thunderbolts, the lightning that sparks our fires, when people do not. All vertebrates share it—in some, it bears the cones and rods of eyes as if it might see and not just sense the presence of light, of even the burned world's luminosity.

Just say a quiet "good-by," my mother writes, and tells us to read "Song" by Christina Rossetti in a *Little Treasury of Great Poetry* on her bookshelf, a gift when my mother was just a girl from my great Aunt Katherine, long dead now. *It will explain how I feel.*

What happens, then, when the eye can no longer see, when the world once transmuted into shape and shapelessness, degradations of light and darkness, flower and cone, goes blank? *When I am dead, my dearest, / Sing no sad songs for me /,* Christina Rossetti writes:

> *I shall not hear the nightingale*
> *Sing on, as if in pain.*
> *And dreaming through the twilight*
> *That doth not rise nor set*
> *Haply I may remember*
> *And haply may forget.*

I look up *haply*: "archaic word for *perhaps*."

Past sunset, the sky burns its fire. Next summer, perhaps, we will be freed from this drought and its smoke. Perhaps not. And, perhaps, my mother will still see, or not, and I'll lead her to stand, not beneath the stars and their little lights where Emerson tells us "man is most alone," but beneath the pines and their flowering cones where Pitys still weeps, and I'll trace my mother's fingers, and my own, around and around the endless spiraling, the naked seeds, seen or unseen.

Orbital Forcing

Last Thursday night, the Spring fire near Lake George finally "contained," and the Waldo Canyon on the far side of Pikes Peak not yet burning—an arsonist's fire.

I sit on my balcony watching the hooked moon vanish behind Grouse or Little Bull Mountain, the twilight's afterglow still "heavenly" with the last particulate vestiges of the Colorado Springs fire. A bat, brown or free-tailed, long-eared, flutters near me, night flying insect-eater zeroed in on one of the dozens of migratory miller moths I shoo into the night.

My daughter has texted me a picture of herself holding a bat up by Nederland at a camp she's attending for a CU biology class. She holds the bat by the tips of its wings, black fan she smiles behind. I have never seen one so close—all wing-crepe of membrane and blood vessel, of thin-boned humerus, radius and ulna, of the hind legs' calcar and keel.

Chiroptera, "hand-wing," the Greeks named this ancient order of mammals extending back to the Eocene period, some fifty-five million years ago, when the earth experienced one of its greatest climate changes, the Paleocene–Eocene Thermal Maximum—the earth's temperature rising six degrees over twenty thousand years. Global warming, of course—sea level changes, a forty thousand year "backflow" current warming the deepest oceans, species forced into extinction. The scientists ponder volcanic activity, comet impact, orbital forcing—cyclical warming caused by the "eccentricity" of earth's elliptical orbit—as causes for this global phenomena that led to a rise in modern mammalians like this bat my daughter will measure, weigh, let nestle against her jeans until finally she holds it to the night and it stutters off, Persephone's underworld companion piercing the night air with the ultrasonic frequencies of echolocation she cannot hear.

"Two years below normal precipitation," the Forest Service spokeswoman will tell us six days later when the Waldo Canyon Fire breaks two containment lines firemen bulldozed and hand-shoveled along the ridge above Mountain Shadows, Colorado Spring's western suburb, and torches enormous houses into fire balls, thirty-two thousand people evacuated along the Garden of the Gods, the Air Force Academy, almost to Interstate 25, what Tom, my cabin neighbor, hopes will be the "ultimate firebreak."

"Five days record-breaking heat above a hundred degrees, sixty-five mile-an-hour erratic winds in the canyon," the Forest Service woman will say.

"Global warming," Leonard will say.

"Arsonist," I'll reply.

I remember the bats swerving over us at the elementary school across the street in Columbine, when the girls were young, barely visible in the darkening evening like disoriented barn swallows, brief sightings in the dark, the girls frightened. Here, the bats day roost in trunk holes and behind the loosened bark of trees I must now be careful not to disturb or in the crevasses of the granite rock that surrounds this cabin. Or in the hundreds of abandoned mines scattered throughout Victor and Cripple Creek, some bats migrating only within state to roost within their "hibernacula," long term roosts where the bats will enter "torpor," their metabolism slowed to help them "sleep" through the coldness of winter in the warmth of mines where once miners abandoned burros, where they died of thirst and hunger a thousand feet beneath the earth in the limitless dark.

With Highway 24 from Colorado Springs closed, my hopes of getting to the cabin the back way through the scorched and bristled pine remnants of the month-long Hayman fire of 2002, when ashes drifted some ninety miles to Denver the day we buried Leonard's mother in her pine box, are, of course, dashed: Woodland Park, integral pathway to the cabin, falls under pre-evacuation orders, my mother begs me by phone not to drive up to the cabin to pull the piled wood scraps from under the deck, to cut the aspen "dog hair," to create the defensible space I need against fire. Twenty fires an arsonist has set throughout Cripple Creek and Divide, each fire, until this one set in Waldo Canyon, discovered and extinguished before any real damage could be done. Red Flag warnings, a total fire ban for the state of Colorado, extended drought conditions, erratic winds: the Waldo Canyon Fire is the ghost of the Hayman Fire, started by a forest ranger named Terry Barton, who claimed to have accidently ignited the fire when she burned the letters of her estranged husband in a fire ring of stones—some of the stones, it was found later, had been pushed away to allow the fire to escape. I drive through 138,000 acres of charred pine and mudslides, where eight lives were taken, each time I drive through the back way along the Platte River and Pike National Forest.

Civil dusk, nautical dusk, astronomical dusk. Mercury, Mars, Saturn burn in the western sky brighter and brighter as the sun drops degree by degree, the ancients would tell me, past the stationary earth. Over a hundred years ago, Victor burned, a fire ignited in a brothel on Paradise Alley. The bats are hunting the night skies—how many lost to the fungus *Geomyces destructans*, white-nose syndrome the Colorado Wildlife Division warns me of, I don't know—and Persephone, earthly, hears still the voices of the dead. Somewhere beyond the coming fire, my daughter and her classmates dip small mammals that cannot fly into fluorescent powder and release them to the dark. And east of me, a still unburnt Colorado Springs illuminates the horizon with its spill light, a faint glow I sometimes mistake for moonrise.

Unearthing Leetso

I could begin here, 9,600 feet above sea level, the aspens burnt red with summer drought, the dark wind of their light caught against the clouded sky, the mountain to the north of me that I still don't know how to name turned inside out for its gold.

When I stand on this finger of glacial granite pointing from our Colorado mountain meadow south and westward, and the evening sky is that preternatural blue of high altitude, and the air I breathe, the gravity anchoring me here, only a thin cusp of well-being beneath the great expanse of dark matter, of black holes, of star stuff that burns in the atoms of my body too, I can see past Nipple Mountain to the Arkansas River Valley shining like a second sky of far off car lights, of cities thinning toward Raton Pass and the New Mexico border I will soon cross over.

I could begin here, but it is on the Navajo Nation, the teachers of the reservation will tell me, that the world begins—*Hahjeenah*, the Emergence.

★ ★ ★

Ron pulls the beaded necklace of my prayer bag over my shirt collar and adjusts it so that I can no longer feel its cool deer bone and black obsidian against my neck. He pats my chest where the white deerskin sewn with a rainbow of glass beads rests. A small, rather endearing man in round black-framed glasses, his touch, I decide, is motherly, fussing.

"Did you bless it?" Ron asks me.

Ron is Navajo, Diné, *the People*. I am driving through the Four Corners of the World in a small Toyota with Ron and two other Diné somewhere between the Sacred Mountains that gods built—*White Shell, Abalone Shell, Blue Bead, Big Mountain Sheep*, the Navajo call them. I invited myself along for this ride to a small Indian gift shop where the Anglo teachers on the reservation have assured me I will find "great prices." We are here as part of an education grant awarded to the University of Northern Colorado to collaborate with Navajo Nation teachers on teaching strategies in American History and Civics. Ron is caretaker for his elderly parents and his sister's children, gladly exchanging his reservation trailer for a few nights in a hotel room. Leroy is a Diné middle school teacher and activist from Rough Rock, Arizona, where girls in home economics take knives to the throats of rams. He will teach us ethnobotony, to pray to the plants that would heal us, if only we might ask. Jennifer, a Diné professor, historian, and author, is my colleague for this project, today a field trip on the history of uranium mining. She is skeptical of me—a white woman, poet but no historian, stranger to the desert and reservation but who was asked to teach teachers to find poetry within the hearts of the Navajo students she will never see.

"Oh, please don't," interjects Jennifer.

It is a year earlier. We are in the midst of planning a workshop on the reservation. I proposed bringing in the skeletons of birds and field mice, the wings of dragonflies, the uprooted teeth of cows, and the craterous skulls of unidentified animals I have hauled from the fields of my childhood as writing aids.

After the first year, Jennifer's protests are predictable. I chafe at her silently until I stand in front of the Navajo teachers and read to them James Wright's poem, "Rain," with its falling eyelids of owls and sad bones of hands descending.

"What does this poem feel like?" I ask naively.

A long silence.

"Death," one teacher whispers. The others stir uneasily in this affront to the life they celebrate—its red rock fluidity, its bird-winged insistence.

"We don't speak of it openly," Jennifer tells me and I think of the stories spoken to me not by the Navajo but by the Anglo historians who visit this reservation with me—of the ancient Acomas attacked by the Spaniards in 1599 on Sky Mesa, the City of Sky, the women throwing their children, themselves from the mesa's rim while the Spaniards cut the captives into pieces, cut the left feet off the old men left to wander in warning. And I think of the desecrated, the scattered bones in the ruins of the Chaco Canyon or Canon de Chelly, Puebloan bones bitten, some say, by the Navajo Ancient Ones who wanted not even the spirit of their dead enemies to walk the earth. I think of the great Navajo grandmothers and grandfathers forced to leave the Sacred Mountains by the U.S. Army, of those who died during the three hundred mile Long Walk of 1864 to Fort Sumner, of the pregnant women who dropped exhausted, full-bellied, to the old sea floor of the Pecos River valley, their half-formed sons and daughters lost to them, their skin like wax melting beneath the desert sun, melting even now beneath my fingers.

The crushed bones of fish and ancient sea creatures blow like dust from the desert sea floor across our windshield. Some- where, Ron tells me, a Navajo woman touches her lips to corn pollen. Somewhere, Navajo families bless the first red flowers of their daughters' menses, and grandfathers and fathers bundle the plucked plumes of eagles and bluebirds they will make holy to protect all who come after them.

"Did you bless it?" Ron asks again, pointing to my prayer bag, and I nod my head, yes, already lying, I realize, like the Anglo I am as he mimes for me the blessings I am too late to give or to receive.

★ ★ ★

"My grandparents say when I was a young girl I would herd the sheep to the high mesa and talk to them like I was Miss Navajo," Victoria says. "I wanted it so much."

She smiles out of her black-framed glasses, her face, like the other Navajo women, round and smooth as a brown berry. She stands close to me. I bend down toward her, utterly conscious of my long limbs that stretch me out almost three heads higher than her.

She stops for a moment, then holds her hands out in front of her, echoing the roundness of a globe.

"I remember holding peaches in my hands. My grandparents grew them." Her fingers squeeze the empty air. "They were so beautiful, so full. But now . . ." She looks at me. "I wonder what I was holding."

We have spent the morning at Diné College in Tsaile, Arizona, at a seminar on the history of uranium mining on the reservation. Because of the United States' nuclear arms race in the 1940s, close to four million tons of uranium ore were mined throughout the Navajo Nation's 27,000 square miles. When the demand for ore weakened, more than one thousand uranium mines were abandoned, riddling the red and yellow sandstones of the reservation like radioactive catacombs. The Navajo, willing workers for the few dollars earned digging out the mines, became the victims of a mass deception by mining executives, the U.S. Government, and even their own Navajo Tribal Council—who knew of the contamination left behind not only in the mines but in the uranium ore left outside them, but were too poor to instigate reclamation projects beyond nailing a few boards across the mouths of the empty mines. So they kept silent.

Victoria and the other Navajo Nation teachers remember playing in the abandoned mines as late as the 1980s. They write journal entries for me about the mines' sweet darkness against the blinding desert heat, the coolness of deep underground waters. Some Navajo families scavenged the mines for the perfectly round plugs, carved out of test stone, to grind their food. Others built their homes out of the waste rock, these "hot" houses of the nomadic scattered unmarked throughout the reservation, and inhabited still. The uranium mines blighted a whole generation ancestral to these teachers with cancers, young sheepherding mothers drinking from the oasis in the desert, formed by the empty tailing pits below the mines, and giving birth to children with club feet, retardation, and weakened immune systems.

A *genetic disorder*, the doctors surmised, *unique only to the Navajo people*.

Victoria shows me a picture of herself as Miss Navajo Nation, essence of the powerful matriarchal figures in Navajo religion: *First Woman, White Shell Woman, Changing Woman*. In traditional Navajo dress of tiered velvet and animal skin moccasins, Victoria is serene and beautiful. Now, she holds her hands to her throat.

"What's the ticking machine called that tests for radiation?" she asks.

"Geiger counter," I tell her. She asks me how to spell it and repeats the letters one by one, her fingers at her throat ticking.

★ ★ ★

What I have in common with the Navajo lies beneath this Colorado granite, red as their volcanic sandstone, erupted here out of the soul of the earth by a mass of glacial ice plowing incrementally across the land some millions of years ago, and in the "glory holes" that dot my mountain meadow, the small and sometimes large craters pick-axed by gold-fevered miners of the 1800s looking for the white and rose veins of quartz where sometimes gold fine as web adhered, and still does today.

In this past year, the price of gold and uranium has skyrocketed. Hundreds of mining claims on the Navajo Nation have been registered for the vast uranium deposits predicted to still sit in the belly of these mines abandoned some thirty year ago, while here, in Colorado, with the third largest deposit of uranium in the country, anxious prospectors have filed, so far, three thousand new mining claims.

In the distance, beyond Bull Mountain, the periodic dynamite blasts for gold roll across the mountain plain where the Cripple Creek & Victor Gold Mining Company still surface mines for gold above the touring retirees. They travel by *Ramblin Express* motor coaches from Colorado Springs to play the slots in Cripple Creek casinos or ride the old mining cages of the Mollie Kathleen Gold Mine one thousand feet into the earth, where men once dug by candlelight and burros hauled stone and gold through the blighted tunnels they would never leave.

★ ★ ★

Ron, Leroy, Jennifer and I pass near the Four Corners Power Plant on our way to the gift shop. Burnt coal shrouds the sky.

"The men pierce themselves," Ron says. "Even the women pierce their upper arms with eagle feathers. Or drape buffalo skulls down their backs."

Jennifer eyes me from the rear view mirror. Once at a dinner, she talked with other Diné teachers about driving off the reservation to buy peyote, the small cactus containing the hallucinogenic mescaline, legalized for ceremonial use by the Navajo Nation. How was the peyote used? I asked her.

"No," she said. "It's Navajo ritual."

Ron invites me to the Hopi and Navajo Sun Dance on Big Mountain for the Fourth of July weekend. He warns me to wear long dresses and, if it is the time of my *moon*, I must excuse myself from the dance and go elsewhere with the other menstruating women.

I stare out the window at the smudged sky. Owned by the Arizona Public Service Company and unregulated because of jurisdiction disagreements, the Four Corners Power Plant is considered one of the "dirtiest plants in the country." The smudge I see, according to the Sierra Club, is the yearly accumulation of "fifteen million tons of sulfur dioxide, nitrogen oxide, particulates and carbon dioxide . . . along with 590 pounds of toxic mercury." Only as recently as 2007, the EPA finalized a clean air "plan" for the Four Corners Power Plant as a result of a lawsuit filed by the Sierra Club.

"Can you see Ship Rock?" asks Leroy, irritated, as all the reservation people are, by the Anglo-owned power plant that darkens their skies. Somewhere ahead looms an ancient volcano eroded by wind into airy striations. Even the name, *Ship Rock*, is a betrayal by white explorers who renamed every stone, butte, and mesa with the names of a world only they could know— *Ship Rock, Church Rock, Window Rock. Tsé Bit'a'í, Rock with Wings,* is what the Navajo call this volcanic vestige that floats across the desert horizon, symbol of the great bird that carried their ancestors. I begin to understand why Navajo activists like Leroy call for "immersion" teaching—only Navajo language, only Navajo knowledge. More than half the Navajo population is comprised of young people under the age of eighteen, Leroy tells me, yet only one-eighth can speak and think in Navajo.

"Grandmother and Grandfather tongue keeps you strong," Leroy says. "When you speak Diné, you speak directly to the holy people. Holy people don't speak English."

An Anglo teacher who once journeyed with a group of Navajos to the United Nations to beg, without success, to be heard on the abandoned uranium mines poisoning them, tells me later that the plume of this power plant and the Great Wall of China were the only man-made objects in the sixties that the first astronauts floating in space could see—forty eight years ago. I try to calculate the total amount of toxins spewed into the reservation air since then, but can't. It is no accident, I soon realize, that this plant, the only one to operate in the United States without a pollution permit, stands on reservation land.

"The men sense it," Ron continues. His round glasses wink at me. "It interferes with the spirits. Sometimes announcements over the loudspeaker ask menstruating women to leave."

Why do men, everywhere, I wonder, find the shedding of cyclical blood so unsettling? *Hozhonji*, blessing or happiness, is the peace one finds through ritual, through the achievement of harmony with the universe. I think of the woman's body waning and waxing so naturally with the constant moon. In ritual then, the men pierce themselves through the chest with a thin knife and insert a bone attached to a long skein of hide tied to a stationary pole. The object is to become unattached. Later, I find an old black and white photo of an Indian, long dead, pierced and leaning back from the pole, waiting for his moment of release, a woman, I imagine, somewhere watching, holding the plumes of an eagle high and bleeding.

★ ★ ★

At Diné College, a moldy air conditioner drones and rattles in the classroom's one window. Called "the most important post-secondary educational institution on the Navajo Nation" by the Navajo Nation Council, Diné College was started as a boarding school by Christians determined to "anglicize" Navajo children. There are reports of humiliation, of physical abuse. None of the teachers I ask, even in my generation taken from their parents and grandparents to these boarding schools scattered across the country by good Christians determined to eradicate the "savage" in them, can remember their early years.

The teachers and I sit in shorts and T-shirts behind large tables. *Rock with Wings* floats above the air conditioner in the dusty corner of the window glass. The presenter of this seminar on the uranium mines is a Diné professor who watched his own father, a miner, linger for six years in a coma and then die from radiation poisoning. He stands in front of us, wearing large green rubber gloves and reminds us that we have to be careful of what substances we bring to our students.

"But this is safe," he says as he waves the tube of a Geiger counter over the uranium ore he's locked in plastic sandwich "baggies." We listen to the slow, steady clicking. "Only background radiation," he explains. "It comes from everywhere—even the stars."

With his green gloves, he passes out the baggies to the teachers. They titter nervously. He became an activist after his father's death, helping to start the Red Mesa / Mexican Water Four Corners Uranium Committee which served as a catalyst for the passage of RECA, the Radiation Exposure Compensation Act, in 1990, *only* thirty-eight years after the last boom in uranium mining on the reservation, *only* thirty years after scientists conclusively realized the connection between radiation and lung cancer. The RECA was amended as recently as 2000 to, among other things, broaden the definition of "eligible" uranium miners to include those who handled the ore and mine waste above ground, and to include, too, the "downwinders"—those unsuspecting citizens who had been physically present downwind of the infamous Nevada Nuclear Test Sites. RECA provides monetary awards to those who contract diseases recognized as a consequence of radiation exposure. The list, according to the U.S. Justice Department's Radiation Compensation Program home page, includes:

> *leukemia (other than chronic lymphocytic leukemia), multiple myeloma, lymphomas (other than Hodgkin's disease), and primary cancer of the thyroid, male or female breast, esophagus, stomach, pharynx, small intestine, pancreas, bile ducts, gall bladder, salivary gland, urinary bladder, brain, colon, ovary, or liver (except if cirrhosis or hepatitis B is indicated), or lung.*

"We have the tendency to destroy ourselves," the professor says. Some Navajo landowners, desperately poor, said "yes" to those mining companies littering the borders of the Navajo Nation now and applying to mine what has already been desecrated. "*In situ* leaching," where corroding substances such as acid are introduced deep into the uranium deposits, allows mining companies to extract more of the ore. While the process is considered less evasive to the surface ground, a report by the WISE project warns that it "releases considerable amounts of radon, and produces certain amounts of waste slurries and waste water during the recovery of the ore from the liquid" which threatens natural groundwater. Hydro Resource Incorporated, a subsidiary of a Dallas-based company, filed to open four new mines near Church Rock, near the sole underground aquifer of roughly

fifteen thousand Navajos living below poverty level. HRI's appli-
cation became a catalyst for the Navajo Nation Tribal Council
passing a uranium ban legislation in 2005, what the Navajo
Nation president begged the U.S. Congress to honor in 2008.

The teachers slide the plastic baggies to each other with
notebooks and pencils, careful not to touch them with their
hands. In a spike of sunlight, the ore shines. I take it out to see
it better—gray rock, stained with what looks like yellow moss.
The "destroyer" in the uranium mines is called "radon daughters," a product of uranium decay. It is what makes the Geiger
Counter click. It is what caused early on the abnormally high
number of lung cancer deaths in the Navajo miners. The Navajo
call uranium, *leetso*, roughly meaning *yellow earth* or *yellow dirt*.
Or *yellow monster*. I put the ore back.

The professor passes out a map from a four-part *LA Times* arti-
cle on uranium and the Navajo Nation by the journalist Judy
Pasternak published in 2007. Red dots—abandoned mines—
flower profusely across it. The map startles the teachers who
live at the heart of those flowers.

"The mines we will see today," he says, gesturing with his
green gloves, "were part of a secret project. People were injected
with radium to see how the body would react to radioactive
material. Seventy-nine of the workers in the test were Navajo.
They were never told about the effects of high exposure."

I find my fingers in my mouth, dusty and bitter from the ore,
and jerk them out.

★ ★ ★

It looks like the flesh of an elephant, the ruptured Colorado
mountain that hosts Cresson Mine, cyanide leaching through
its veins, through the thin shale of earth with its white heart
of quartz and clinging gold. Rocks spill down the sides of the
mine, caught above the road by a timber "cribbing" of old logs

miners in the late 1800s used to catch the dump rock of the Mary McKinney mine. The Cripple Creek & Victor Gold Mining Company wants to cut forty acres of trees above Cripple Creek in order to strip-mine the area. They promise that the expansion and the cyanide, sent into the ground to leach tiny particles of gold from the rock, won't bring harm to the ground water. I have never thought much of the mines below the surface here— only of the startlingly bareness of the stripped mountain, the plumb line of broken rock spewed out from the inside of it, or of the ruins of lost mining cities like Independence, their tattered miners' homes once strewn through the back gully wash of mountains, the rusted machinery of their mines that drove a nail into the heart of the earth—benign, I wonder now? The process of leaching is the same for uranium or gold: arsenic, cyanide or other poison sent into the ground to separate what is precious from what is not. When we drilled for our water, I imagined only the purest water submerged beneath shale rock and granite for eons and millenniums, sacred water untouched by time or slow erosion. I try to remember what they called the disease of Navajo babies born deformed to the women who drank contaminated run-off from the uranium mines, or ground corn with pestles made from the core of mined test rock, smashing their grain with radioactive rock for decades.

★ ★ ★

We travel by Greyhound to Cove, Arizona, where the mining boom of the 1940s began. We pass Mexican Cry Mesa, where once Navajo warriors rolled down boulders and logs to kill their enemies, the Mexican women heard weeping in the evenings at the bottom of the mesa for their dead. I watch the sandstone roll past the Greyhound window, the shadows of its mines, its weeping red rust.

"'*Only Widows Live Here*'," the professor tells us, Cove's

nickname and testament to the devastation wrought by the waste dumped from thirty uranium mines right across from the Cove Day School. We stand in the empty road, a few houses, the school, scattered around us. The professor holds the Geiger counter close to the road, to the scrub at the side of it, to the cattle guard we walk over.

"Before anyone could clean it up," he says, "they built the road over it."

We listen to the anxious rise and fall of the Geiger counter. A slight wind weaves around us, picks at the mess of sheared sheep wool at our feet. A single crow flies past. Two teenage boys walk past us down the road. It's said that twice as many young American Indian males commit suicide than in any other racial group and, in one study, fifteen percent of those surveyed—nine hundred and seventy-one high school Navajo children—reported attempted suicides. Today, Navajo teenagers living below mines reportedly have cancer rates seventeen times above the national average. I watch the boys, the age of my daughters, waver in the heat, then disappear.

No sound now but the Geiger counter. The valley sandstone reddens and twists in the failing light. The professor warns us of the toxic chemicals seeping into the soil and the surface waters across the reservation. I squint through my camera lens, looking for the mouths of abandoned mines. The teachers I am with, half-laughing, take turns holding the tube of the Geiger counter to their throats, listening for the radiation that causes thyroid cancer, and I wonder why I have come here.

★ ★ ★

The tiny Indian gift shop appears innocuously at the side of the highway. A few small glass cases hold beautiful works of silver and turquoise, beads, and weavings. I am overcome with greed.

I pile pieces to buy on the counter, including the single white-skin prayer bag. Jennifer debates between a bracelet and a small piece of hand weaving. Ron and Leroy join us, eyeing the small sticker prices on each piece of jewelry I've piled in a heap on the counter. The 21st Navajo Nation Council cites 2000 Census figures of fifty-six percent living below poverty level and per capita incomes of $5,599. Power lines float above the scattered homes and trailers of the Navajo, but they carry their electricity off the reservation, leaving many Navajo families in the dark with kerosene lanterns. While millions of gallons of reservoir water are pumped through underground pipes throughout the west to coastal cities, many Navajo must drive to community wells to fill plastic containers with water for themselves and their live-stock. Ron, Leroy, and I watch the numbers ring up on the cash register, and I push some of the jewelry away.

"Right now," says Ron, checking his watch as we head toward Montezuma Creek where the teachers are already conducting water experiments to test for pollutants, "the women are holding a Squaw Dance." I look at him expectantly.

"They're probably blackening themselves now. They'll ride horses bareback in circles, chant songs, then take whatever object—clothing, even a hair—they've taken from the one who has given them bad spirit and shoot it."

I look out at the desert, white-washed in the sun, and wonder what the women blacken themselves with. The Squaw Dance seems to be closely entwined with the Enemyway ceremony, designed, I find out later, to absolve contact with non-Nava-jos—me—and stems from earlier war ceremonies that exorcised "ugly things." I think of Jennifer's look in the rear view mirror and wonder about Ron's veracity to me, the Anglo.

Though little has been said, I have sensed friction between the Navajo and Anglo teachers on the reservation that goes beyond

Jennifer's and my clash of personalities, especially on the issue of Navajo immersion in the reservation schools. I ask Jennifer what her views are on immersion and the Anglo's sense of alienation in the Navajo schools. She is silent for a moment, and then looks at me in the rear view mirror.

"This gives you just an inkling of what we have to deal with as Navajo people when we constantly have to deal with foreign history in the classroom. When you're teaching here, you're on our turf. This is our land. Our history. Our culture. I ask them, 'Are you going to support us? Be compassionate?' Have some heart, I tell them."

At Sand Island along the San Juan River outside Bluff, Utah, Jennifer and I take refuge amidst sparse cottonwood trees while the rest of the teachers lunch in the covered picnic area. Another teacher joins us and soon, surprisingly, Jennifer and I laugh over the shared perils of menopause. Nearby, a group of Anglo and Navajo teachers spontaneously perform their rap poem on uranium, *Leetso*, written in English and Navajo.

★ ★ ★

At Montezuma Creek, Utah, tamarisk and Russian olive trees, foreign invaders, suck at the scarce river water. The teachers test for pollutants. Victoria and her husband, a young Navajo police officer, gamely pull on green waders and walk slowly toward the middle of the river where the faster current makes the river pure. Before Victoria would marry her husband, he had to fulfill two requests: wait five years, and build her a "female" Hogan, a traditional round Navajo house described in the *Blessingway*, an ancient creation song.

"It's like a womb," Victoria tells me. "And the man walks into it."

Water smooths the colored rocks and pebbles at my feet. Victoria and her husband stand in the middle of the river, swaying

precariously in the hidden current. I look past them at the sandstone that ruptures the blue skin of the sky, and think of the two
hundred and thirty-seven uranium mines abandoned around
Cove, of the snow and rain that leach through the radioactive
tailings left above ground, of the young mothers, long dead
now, who herded their sheep through the desert, thankful for
the water they found. From what boarded mine, through what
abandoned tailings, does this water run?

Victoria and her husband hold hands now. Victoria's face glows
against the sun for the pictures the other teachers take for them.
She and her husband have four children and want many more.

"Smell the water," one teacher yells. Victoria's husband bends
down low, his hands cupped beneath the surface of the river like
a baptismal bowl, and drinks.

★ ★ ★

Wind. It lets loose before the front, muffles the dynamite blasts
near Cripple Creek, Colorado. Clouds from the southwest slowly
head like a great shadow over me. The aspen leaves turn white,
snap in the wind. It's hard to bear, the wind, to bear this—a
force knocking against your body, not continuous but in great
waves that take your breath away. The body feels dried out,
assaulted, battered. On winter nights, I have held my palms
against the cabin wall and marveled at the stillness inside, the
lack of seeping cold even in the harshest wind. But such tightness
has its drawbacks. We live above a uranium bed, my husband
tells me. A radon test registers nine points, five above what is
considered safe background radiation. In Teller and Park coun-
ties, foreign-owned companies have bought the mineral rights
for tens of thousands of acres of land. In Hartsel, a mountain
subdivision where we once had considered building our cabin,
a uranium company notified landowners that it will explore up

to three thousand acres for mining purposes on what these landowners thought was private land. Few in Colorado have mineral
rights, which means that the land we walk on, build on, is not
ours and subject to the whims of untraceable foreign and domestic companies. I look at the glory holes on our forty acres and
think of our joke to throw away any nugget of gold we might
find so that the drilling companies don't come knocking. Near
Canon City, just south of here below Phantom Canyon, the
Cotter uranium mill applies to the state to reopen and expand.
Before its closure in the '70s, those who ran Cotter mill threw its
tailings into unlined pits and contaminated the drinking water of
a whole subdivision, earning the federal designation of a Super-
fund site, an extreme environmental hazard. A spokesperson for
the company is quoted as saying he hopes citizens will realize
not only how far technology has come in improving mine safety
but how responsibly the company recently acted in containing
the radioactive plume of water leaking from its storage tanks
and contaminating the ground water beneath a local golf course.

Everything here becomes a microcosm of the reservation.

★ ★ ★

"We need to sing and pray more," Leroy says. "The plants will
listen."

The primordial volcanic spires and cones of the Valley of the
Gods jut across the desert floor below, spirits of warriors frozen
within them, the Navajo say. Leroy's ethnobotany lesson trans-
forms weeds and scrub into Indian Rice Grass, Four Wing Salt
Brush, Scorpion Weed. He points to a weed with a white flower.

"Jimson weed," he says, "he white flower that Georgia O'Keefe
painted. Don't touch it. It can kill you."

The teachers say their goodbyes. Most choose not to travel
on past Mexican Hat, Utah, to the Mexican Hat Disposal Cell

located, predictably, a mile or so into the Navajo reservation. Here, 1.3 million tons of tailings and other waste were hauled from the Monument Valley for processing. I hug Jennifer awkwardly, aware as she pats me that I am probably transgressing boundaries.

An Anglo teacher points to my prayer bag. "Did Leroy and Ron give you corn pollen for that?"

I shake my head "no," too awkward to ask them to give me what I know is sacred.

"Here," Leroy says, and pulls out a tiny plastic pouch of corn pollen with a five-dollar sticker on the side of it. Ron opens my prayer bag and puts the pouch in.

"Do you know how to ward off bad spirits with it?" he asks.

"No," I say.

★ ★ ★

We cross the San Juan River, curve around red rock, then pull down a dirt road to what looks like a lake silver beneath the clouded sky. Against it, in the far background, is the Navajo Rift, a stunning monument to the turbulence of time and geology, stone heaved from wind, river and pressure into accordion waves, what the San Juan River has carved into for tens of thousands of years. This "Navajo Blanket," as the Navajo call it, is startlingly red against the vast pit of gray rock of the Mexican Hat Disposal Cell.

"The tailings were my sandbox," Victoria tells me. She has followed us up to the disposal cell, unable to let this go. Though the Navajo Abandoned Mines Land Reclamation Program plugged approximately half of the identified poisonous mines, exposed uranium ore waste rock remains. This is the rock that made up Victoria's childhood "sandbox." But despite the glaring yellow hazard signs and the barbed fence around the processing site, this disposal cell is more benign, our Diné professor reassures us, than the exposed uranium waste rock and fine particulates of Victoria's "sandbox." The disposal cell is made up of thick layers of sand, clay, gravel, and "riprap" designed to eliminate the shedding of radon particles from the 4.4 million dry tons of radioactive uranium waste it covers here. For a thousand years, the professor tells us, the radioactive materials will stay safe beneath this "cap."

"Then the new world will have to figure out what to do," he says. I discover later that the waste, radium-226, has a half-life of approximately 1,620 years, meaning that in 1,620 years, or— if generations go by seventy years—more than twenty-three generations from now, only half the lethal radiation will have dispersed from the site.

I take a picture of Victoria next to the hazard signs. She smiles sweetly into the camera. A hundred yards behind her, propped up on the gray rock, a small stone memorializes the Utah man who willed his body to science. He began his afterlife decomposing in a lawn chair so that scientists could measure the effects of the radiation that seeped out of this engineered "cap" into his dead bones.

Same as the stars, the scientists will tell me.

Leetso, Yellow Monster.

I open my prayer bag, take out the five-dollar bag of corn pollen, kiss it, then begin what Ron and Leroy have taught me— the long bow to the earth and to the fragile self.

You must go back again beneath
the secret places of the earth

—Homeric Hymn 2 to Demeter

Finding the Well

It is the height of the drought. Early spring imperils the scarce snow pack. Reservoirs leach into the strangled air. Dark ash from the Hayman Fire sears the sky over our Littleton suburb. A dowdy woman steps from her Nissan and greets us: "Hi, I'm Ruth. Your water witch."

"Around here . . . ," the water driller stops and looks slyly at his twin, "wild cats just hang from the trees."

"Yeah," says his brother, looking me up and down as I shiver in the morning cold, shouldering my single-man REI tent that I brought for the night. "Get out the barbeque and grill a few steaks while you're at it."

It has been five months since Ruth. *Here* is 9,600 feet above sea level, off Phantom Canyon in the shadow of Nipple Mountain, named by some gold-fevered miner pick-axing his monkish way through a granite glory hole. Sangre de Cristo, Continental Divide, Pikes Peak, Arkansas River Valley—we can see it all from our stunted thicket of boney aspen perched on a knob of mountain meadow.

The air fills with a chalky spew of granite. The drill bit grinds three hundred feet beneath us. The twenty-year cabin dream of two teachers depends on this—finding water. The twin drillers grin at me through the dust of dinosaur bones. Well, why not at thirteen bucks a drill foot, and the unexpected sport of scaring a city lady?

I step back, tripping over the orange-tailed stake Ruth stabbed into the aspen roots. For three years, Leonard and I camped here with our daughters through the droughty summers—even in July, the midnight air cold and heavy against our scalps. "A star-crossed convergence," Leonard and I liked to say, his finding this site on the Internet the same day I took a chance drive up the old 1894 Florence & Cripple Creek Railway.

"Three hundred and forty feet," the drill whines.

Water. The cast of fate. Leonard and I soon numbed to the eager stories of dry wells and missed crevices. Religiously, we researched geology, the science of fissure and watershed. Analysis. Synthesis. Evaluation. The great hallmarks of our advanced degrees. Which U.S. certified, Colorado School of Mines graduate, computer-aided geologist would we choose?

"Here," Ruth says. Her copper rods cross in the wind. I watch her thumbs closely, ready to call off the whole theatrics with their slightest twitch. "Two underground streams cross right here." She points at our favorite aspen and we grimace. "Okay," she says, moving a few feet away. "Here."

I look doubtfully at Leonard.

"This water witch was cheaper," he mouths.

I remember his words as the specter of PCP pipe fastened to the mouth of our only spring looms before me. Dowsing is an ancient art, I reassure myself, of willow and witch hazel, brass and copper. It is depicted, solidly, world-wide, over thousands of years in the drawings of men and women of all cultures divining the will of gods—with a stick.

Four hundred and fifty feet. I contemplate the need for water, the need to leave our tidy suburban house and traverse the skirts of Pikes Peak to a place of lone hawks and reluctant neighbors and the scat of mountain lions and ghost grizzlies that haunt us into bearing whistles and, maybe, the air guns of Bronco fans, or my mother's twelve gauge.

Suddenly, it is silent. Four hundred and sixty feet. Water. Twenty gallons a minute water. The twins cap off the well with a temporary spigot, take my check, and climb into their trucks. Their last farewell jabs hang in the air.

I sit on the wellhead. The six thousand dollar wellhead. Blue-birds plumb and level around me. The notched aspens sing with their nested young, and the sky is white in this soft hour of June darkness.

Ruth hands me her copper rods. They are cold and weighted. I poise myself as light-thumbed as a girl before the Ouija board and its slow spelling out of some far fantastic love.

"Here," Ruth says. "Feel the power."

On White Space and Silence

White space begins this way: I point to the rusted head frames of Battle Mountain, the skeletal portals of abandoned mine shafts—so many invisible but for the names printed on this tourist map—*Sweat Mine, Dead Shot Claim, Smuggler*—and Leonard says, "Who cares." Or I say, here, a sabotaged cable broke, here, fifteen men free falling a thousand feet down in a metal cage past telluride ore and vein to die, and Leonard waves his hands at the ruins scattered across Vindicator Valley, at the junked-out shacks and modular homes that litter Goldfield, and says, "I don't care."

But I do.

And so I say, here, a man named Harry Orchard, over a hundred years ago, rigged dynamite with trip wire—the first man in history to kill without being in the presence of what he killed, to sever flesh from spirit completely blind to its flash into holy. And I want to say to Leonard now, do you see how that word *holy* means everything, but I can't say why exactly, so I say nothing or I say *here*, and this is where that white space comes in, because now I am really thinking *there*, of that long ago girl in Ohio I once saw leaning over a quadriplegic's wheelchair, my father, even doctor that he was, shaking his head at the tiny stain of blood on the back of her stretch pants, a whole unspeakable world I did not know mapped out for me.

★ ★ ★

What is white space? And why should the lyric essayist care about it as much as the poet? To the beginning poet, we say, "Well, white space is everything on the page unmarked," and we point to the left and right margins of the poem, to the empty spaces at the ends of lines and between stanzas.

"This matters as much as what is written," we'll say.

And that is enough, to begin with.

But white space is more than that. It is the power of juxtaposition, of the poet's unspeakable, of the mind moving between what is known and unknown and then back again, that movement mapped out by what the poet Robert Bly calls the "absolute essentiality of image." It is why Ezra Pound can compare passengers at a train station to petals on a branch and we know it. Or why the poet James Wright can touch, in "A Blessing," the ear of a horse, then break into blossom, and we believe him without another word said, only the white space left. Or why I can stand here with Leonard at this scarred foot of Battle Mountain with its hidden portals and horizontal drifts of underground mining tunnels, and be struck so suddenly by the stained pants of a girl I saw only once when I was a child.

★ ★ ★

Essayists speak of the "vertical movement" of the essay, the movement "that delves deeper rather than moving forward," this verticality achieved through "associative memory, figures of speech, lyrical descriptions." What they speak of is the white space Bly calls the "underground passages of association," the intersections of consciousness and unconsciousness. But the difference here is that this white space is made up of what the poet cannot readily say, or does not want to say, like that unnamed image plunging forever into the stalled heart of Rilke's panther.

And it is this, the essential "unsayable" of a poem, understood on an intuitive emotional level, that poets welcome as the white space that can emerge around the perimeters of image and not feel the impetus to delve into it with the essayist's "narrative inquiry," as long as the core of that white space resides where, as Bly says, some "genuine grief has reached out and touched [them]."

I think of the rocks I polished as a girl, tumbling them week after week with finer and finer grit until finally I could keep wholly visible what once only water briefly uncovered: their veins and shadows, the glittering quartz of their unspeakable hearts—my mother's and father's, I am thinking now. In *The Art of the Poetic Line*, James Longenbach says that finally line break means nothing in a poem except how it connects to sentence and syntax. Yet I keep seeing that white space at the line's end dangling there, perilously, as full of want and ruin at the breath's end as I think I was, my parents loving me I know now, but so silent in my childhood landscape of absence and white space, in my own stain that filled it, as I waited for word, for their any word, to name me back into being.

★ ★ ★

Absence. Perhaps this is the word I seek, how white space in the lyric essay, all it so easily says to me in its unsaying because of all my family could never say, might supersede anything else, giving way to neither line, nor break, nor syntax. How beneath everything I am writing here is absence: like that slab of inarticulate rock I hauled out of the Ohio creek bed, when my father was dying, to mount it to the wall outside my cabin door, each time with my entering and leaving this place rubbing my fingers against the blue map of its fossils in the same way Leonard touches the mezuzah affixed to the right of our door in blessing.

Blues, Browns, Walkers, Smiths, Cutlers, Hutzels: I say the names of those who inhabited my childhood landscape as if in litany, and suddenly, here is the girl's menstrual-stained pants, here, my father, uncomfortable with anything of the body, catching my eye, shaking his head in silence at the whole sadness of that scene—all this past and gone, half-guttural what I sometimes pull out of absence, out of white space, out of this stone I keep polishing the silence of with my passing hands.

★ ★ ★

Semiotics teaches us that reality is but a system of signs. That the signified is "the pointing finger," not the "star," only the word. And meaning? The interior construct of the perceiver. I think of the image, and of the skull's bony orbit, and of the eye the pure world enters reversed, upturned through the shaft of its pupil. In gold mining, I tell Leonard, there are two kinds of gold, like there are two kinds of image. One is native or pure, the noble metal of alchemists who sought the philosopher's stone to change what was base into immortal, the "Shining Dawn" of gold's Latinate chemical symbol, of nuggets and dust, of placer deposits and prehistoric alluvial riverbeds, of fossilized veins and fevered prospectors. The visible gold of the hand, I say, like the visceral image we take in that mirrors the concrete world, its worth weighed against the pitiless sun, *there*, I say to Leonard, pointing above the Sangre de Cristo Mountains, the *Blood of Christ*, I say. And Leonard yawns.

Is this the ultimate tension for the lyric essayist: what is written on the page versus all that is not? Articulated word for the willful husband versus all the weight of association, of white space, of absence that she knows dangles after? I say the name of a mountain to Leonard and he yawns, even as this translation of light I am speaking of falls upon the lit stones for me like sacrificial blood, and here is the holy again, and here, Harry Orchard, forgiven and baptized, living forty-six years in an Idaho Penitentiary amongst his chickens and roses, and, here, the woman Harry made widow, who forgave him everything, and here, the man, the boy that I cannot, my unspoken languishing here as if holy to me.

"What do you mean, '*cannot*?'" asks Leonard. "Forgive? Then say that."

* ★ ★ ★

There is a second kind of gold, I tell Leonard, an impure gold wedded to underground metals, to low grade ore, the telluride gold of Cripple Creek and Victor deep in the solidified remains of this volcanic magma we stand over. Elusive gold, I tell him, like that second kind of image, that whole cities of men once lowered themselves thousands of feet down in metal ore buckets to mine, gold unknowable to the eye, gold of the white space, of the vertical, the miner's gold that cyanide and acid dissolve in pits beneath the broken rock until it emerges shining in its half-articulations.

It is this second kind of image, this harder image to mine poets call the "deep image" which can conjure up white space and all its unspoken. Bly calls it "an animal, native only to the imagination," because now the image can never be returned to the world as it once was, but only as an amalgamation of thing and self. This deep image is like the image taking root in the heart of Rilke's panther, in the white space inside it, its fine thin scars spreading out hungrily each passing year—here, Jack the quadriplegic drunk and weeping in his wheelchair, here, the thick yellow molasses of his catheter, here, the girl leaning over him bleeding as I soon would be, my girlhood taken from me—"taken" the insufficient word here—on an early winter afternoon by a stranger spotted later at a bar, a Band Aid on his finger where I had bitten him, spotted there by the brother of Jack who would too soon on a winter night try to touch me through my winter coat with his cold hands—

"Does the infinite space / we dissolve into, taste of us then?" asks the poet Rilke.

* * *

I remember my father, some time later, cutting a black mole from the rickety pipe of my child spine, my father, who loved me so much in his white surgical coat, wanting to heal me. And what I never told Leonard, rooted here with me above these long winding drift tunnels, these abandoned mines and their incessant verticalities: how the blue stone of a world can enter the white space of any of us at any time, my father placing the mole in a glass jar of formaldehyde beneath the operating table's light so we could see its glittering white root stems and the dark melanin of my body he wanted to prove benign, and his, and my mother's, long silence after.

"Say it," Leonard tells me.
   Forgive.

Middens

The packrat moved in last summer after the monsoons we had all prayed for failed. It was a summer of fire. The Teller County arsonist had already lit thirteen quarter–acre fires in three days, and a meteor—"balls of fire," reported the astounded witnesses as far as New Mexico—grounded the air tankers over the Springer fire in late June. Then flames towered two hundred feet up over Waldo Canyon, the air singed orange for days above the ashes and the human remains eventually found in Mountain Shadow.

It was then I first saw the pinecones and the leaf litter ringing the porch board knothole directly beneath the old rocking chair that I once nursed my daughters in. Scanty, but a precise halo. I remember looking up as if the wind could be a god, step out of a paleo-sky and arrange this perfection of detritus like some Tibetan monk sand painting the "world in harmony." But the world in flames, I swept the porch bare.

★ ★ ★

In 1975, two years before I graduated from a small town high school where football rivals dubbed us "River Rats," *Newsweek* heralded "ominous signs that the Earth's weather patterns [had] begun to change dramatically." Concerned scientists pointed to declining growing seasons, rising equatorial temperatures, increased Northern Hemisphere snow cover, "the most devastating outbreak of tornadoes ever recorded," and a significant change in the amount of sunlight that was hitting the earth. The apparently cooling earth. Since 1940, the world temperature had in fact cooled, the "average ground temperatures in the Northern Hemisphere," the National Oceanic and Atmospheric Administration (NOAA) reported, "by half a degree."

"Melt the Arctic ice cap," the Chicken Littles of the time advised. "Cover it with black soot."

Even my mother remembers the deep Ohio freeze that year. My father, a general practitioner, would drive down our gravel lane alongside the county cemetery each morning to reach his city office before winter broke that first frozen tip of light. I think of him checking the breath and pulse of countless patients he might have healed, or not, while my mother worked our farm alone. That winter, she had to sledgehammer apart the milky rills of ice in the water troughs that thickened by morning, and then again by evening, despite the water heaters we floated.

"That year," she says, "twenty-five degrees below zero. Days, I think."

What I remember is my sister and brother and me maneuvering the unwieldy blocks of ice from the troughs, how the freezing water burned through our mittens, while the steamy breath of Angus cows blurred our frozen world. And then, evenings, before the aluminum farm gates lit up with my father's returning headlights, how we had to walk into the dark to pull the ice again, my father, pale in the dashboard light, driving blindly past us out of a precarious world we didn't quite know yet, but for the stones placed over the cold hearts of our neighboring dead.

Headlines or not, this was what we lived.

★ ★ ★

Thirty-seven years later, my mother frail—"She's turned a corner," my brother warns me—my daughters, whom we once ferried newly born through the new snow, grown, and my father, not that frozen world of my childhood, dead, the headlines repeat themselves, but with a twist. Yes, changing weather patterns, rising surface temperatures, "Frankenstorms," and "historic tornado outbreaks," but spawned, it seems, not by a cooling Earth this time, but a warming one, this world rife now with open Arctic water, loss of summer sea ice, and Greenland's Petermann Glacier calving for the second time in three years a forty-six square mile chunk of ice, two times the city of Manhattan, while fires in the west burn and we grieve what's lost. And what's soon to be lost.

"Global warming," my husband Leonard and the news say, "accelerated by human activity," even as scientists report the ending of an eleven-year solar cycle, the most active in eight thousand years, thus the sun increasing, even more than it always has, its spew of flares and spots, solar radiation that NOAA now says "drives the weather machine" and what Mayan occultists say foretell the "killer" solar flares of cosmic alignment, prophesized some five thousand years ago to ignite this world into destruction, or renewal, just two days ago.

I don't know what to believe.

My mother, visiting from the Ohio retirement home she lives in now, clasps my elbow each time we walk outside, ice or sun. I ask her, as if she were my blind and shrinking Tiresias, what she thinks.

"I really don't know what to think. Or to do," she says, and I carefully hold her arm, so thin now, closer to me.

★ ★ ★

Midden is a Middle English word that comes from an old Norse word, *mykdyngja,* a combination of *dung* and *manure pile.* Think refuse, kitchen sink, paleological trash heap. An ancient domestic pile of bones, shells, whatever an ancient people used, and coprolites that archeologists study to know a dead people.

Or a packrat.

Or a world.

I think of Leonard and his online compatriots, intent in their basements learning the most recent stats for global warming— "Ninety-eight percent of scientists believe in it," Leonard tells me—how they would scoff at my apparent ignorant willfulness, worrying as I do over global warming and the predictions of every spokesperson, scientist or not, who tells me how my world will burn and end, or freeze and end. Yet there is that ice age of my childhood, and my half-memories of illustrated texts implicating cold-blooded, tail-brained dinosaurs in some kind of non-maternal expulsion, their young chipping themselves free from eggs untended, deserted, this the first of a whole litany of bitter disillusionments—my father dead, my mother soon blind—I cannot get over.

Samuel Arbesman, a scholar and expert in scientometrics, the "science of measuring the 'quality' of science," claims that just as there is a half-life to a radioactive isotope, there is a half-life to knowledge, the bulwark of "facts" we frail humans hunker against in the chaos of the unknown.

What is that half-life?

Forty-five years, unless, as I want to point out to Leonard, it is a fact published in a taxpayer-funded Louisiana school biology textbook proclaiming dinosaurs sunned themselves alongside Noah on the gopher wood of the Ark.

So I don't know what to believe.

Or I don't want to believe, the way I don't want to believe that a cabin built in the midst of an aspen grove could cause a kill-off of whole colonies of aspen, or disrupt the migration patterns of elk herds that more and more rarely graze in view of our windows. Or that now in December, in the midst of what the news calls "this historic drought," after feet of snow and sub-zero temperatures, last summer's Fern Lake mountain fire—its genesis human—still smolders in remote pitchy loam unburned for eight hundred years.

★ ★ ★

All night, after I swept the porch bare that first time, the dogs slept restless beneath the cracked window, the summer air heavy with its soot. The next morning, the little god-collage had returned, this time spreading to the other rocking chair, knuckles of pine-cone and bark poised around a second knothole. And this time, little brown pellets clustered on my welcome mat.

Packrat or Woodrat, the field guide read, *classification in the rodent genus.*

White-throated or white-toothed, dusky-footed or big-eared, bushy-tailed or not, a rat. Despite its koala bear visage and its penchant for the shiny foil of Hershey's Kisses.

"A rat," my mother repeated over the phone last summer, still feeling well. "A big rat." And then, not surprisingly, given her farm girl upbringing, she added, "Just shoot it," and laughed.

★ ★ ★

Environmental interloper. Destroyer of aspen trees and middens my packrat resurrects each morning for my persistent sweepings. Self-professed global warming cynic, despite the fires that still burn in the valleys, singeing our sun red. I don't know what to do.

Dave, our mountain man rancher and professed killer of

wildcats—"Seven or eight," he tells me, "shot right out of the trees"—visits on a Caterpillar with tires sized for lunar landscapes and shakes his head when I show him the packrat signs. He pulls a long-nosed revolver from the cab toolbox, a gun I faintly remember from a collection of a past boyfriend, son of a sheriff deputy who each winter night, when the plows towered snow over the Iowa streets, no global warming there, tucked his weighty magnum beneath our bed sheets against what, I don't know. Dave warns me of engine block stowaways, incised carburetor wires.

"Mess with my truck and I will hunt you down," he warns my hidden packrat.

Leonard and I visit the neighbors near Eight Mile Creek, waterless now for the first time anyone can remember in this high plains ranching land dissected into forty and fifty fenced acres. "Responsible hunters," our neighbors describe themselves. They follow the Forest Service guidelines for bow or rifle hunting, kill only what they are allowed, skin, then butcher the carcasses for their own consumption. The heads of their elk and deer hang from their walls, the largest clad in Santa Claus hats.

"Oh," they lament in unison, describe the packrat that homesteaded beneath their gas grill, the mysterious pounds of pinto beans she towed in each night. Even the hunters do not want to kill the packrat— "so cute, really,"—and describe a complex arrangement of bungee cords and the elevation of the gas grill that finally sent the packrat packing, only after she had eaten the roots of their Himalayan tomato plants seeded so carefully within their water towers.

I buy a live animal trap at the Ace Hardware in Cripple Creek. Little known packrat fact: packrat middens can grow up to five feet high and last for fifty thousand years, cemented together by what's called "amberat," the viscous urine of the packrat. In western Utah, scientists found in one midden the still preserved bone of a camel extinct on this continent for 12,500 years. That pile of pinecones, that halo as I called it beneath our rocking chairs? A packrat midden, evidenced by the tiny gold droplets I've lately noticed crystallized on our windowsill.

Leonard holds out a vanilla wafer. "Everyone likes vanilla wafers," he says, and carefully reaches into the metal cage to load the trigger spring. All night I worry: an accidental broken neck, the packrat exposed to the elements in this metal cage and frozen, despite Leonard's warnings of global warming. My daughter over the phone confirms this likely outcome, describing the hypothermic death of voles in the metal traps she helped place overnight in the high summer mountains during her week of scientific study. The next morning, the trap is sprung and, of course, empty, our pristine wafer debauched by a nibble.

Meanwhile, the packrat's midden expands in piles along the cracks of the porch boards, deepens beneath the rocking chairs.

Across the nation, in what was called the hottest summer in history, nine million acres burned, a record set only three times before. Down in the valleys, Colorado held funerals for the six dead and burned, this fire season called by our governor "the worst in history." January, and the red flag warnings continue. Already we fear the coming summer and its probable drought.

I remember after 9/11 how the Tibetan monks constructed a mandala, a sand painting at the Smithsonian museum, a rite of healing, they said. Then they destroyed it, a reminder of the world's and our impermanence. At its simplest, a mandala, like my porch halo, is a circle, organic or inorganic, "a cosmic diagram," I read, "that reminds us of our relation to the infinite, the world that extends both beyond and within our bodies and minds."

Once my mother and I passed hordes of Canadian geese amassed in a great circle where winter ice melted from a lake. My mother remembered the first time we saw a Canadian goose fly over our Ohio farm, its high blaring call sending her running, bird guide in hand, to the dam of the lake to watch the steady oars of its wings dip over the fields, until finally it was only a small echo in the ear. I remembered my father, still alive one early autumn morning when I had not known he would so early die in less than three months, his brain wasted by "plaques" and "tangles." He sat on a wooden bench my mother bought from Home Depot and set in their new backyard by a bulldozed lake so he could remember the farm she had sold to be nearer to my brother—the bench I took from her and keep now above the circle of aspens near our cabin. A keepsake of that day the geese blurred the air around him, my father already a stillness in the world's flurry we could not touch.

There are two kinds of fossils. Body fossils are the actual parts of the body left behind by the dead—their hair or their scales, their bones, their little chips of enamel. Trace fossils are the small tracks we leave behind in the earth, the places we have called our own, the dams of lakes, a fifteen yard creek of flat stones and clay between the fence lines of a farm we once loved, the woven bird nest we leave on top of a pair of cow horns to grace a barnyard where once we stood in the cold dark, our father already driving past us and our mother waiting. It is said that "one single animal can make thousands and thousands of traces in its lifetime, but it will only leave behind one body when it dies."

"Have you gotten rid of it yet?" my mother asks me over the phone. She is concerned about disease, about the viscous urine that I've told her scientists study from ancient middens for its record of rainwaters and the isotopes of cosmic particles that fall down upon us from whole solar systems, whole eternities we do not yet know.

Along the cabin's deck, beautiful circular patterns of pine needles appear. Wind? Packrat? I do not touch them.

* * *

Today, I am wondering about the exactitude of science, the
science of climate change, to be precise. "We're toast," James
Hansen proclaimed, NASA scientist who first sounded the global
warming alarm back in 1988, choosing a record seven day period
of one hundred degrees plus temperatures in Washington D.C.
to fortuitously present decades of scientific findings to a sweating
Congress and a wondering public. The concept of global warming went global, despite scientists' own disclaimer: "Weather is
not climate. It's disingenuous to link the two."

Now NOAA's 2012 Arctic Report Card records the lowest
"sea ice extent" since satellite observation began in 1979 and
record-breaking "near-ice sheet-wide surface melting" in Greenland, both conditions, NOAA points to, as indicators of the
continued real impact of thirty years of global warming. Yet
in Antarctica, there is a significant increase of sea ice, and the
"snow extent" in the Northern Hemisphere has been at record
highs. And this past January, Arctic ice increased at a "slightly
higher average for the month," according to the National Snow
and Ice Data Center, a fact I'll cling to.

Paleoclimatologists, the scientists who study past climates,
study climate change through what they call "proxy," a word I
look up, which means "the authority or power to act for another."
They study the trace fossils of the earth, the hardened midden
where extinct grass pollen once blew into it with the wind, the
rings of trees to mark the rains that bring growth, the growth
bands of coral, the bore holes and the ice cores they drill for
ancient signs of heat and cold, so few the ways to know the
world that existed before us, except in the little signs it gives us,
its substitutions.

A study of southwestern Ponderosa Pine and tree rings to determine the connection between sustained drought and the "mega fires" of the past years reveal that fifteen hundred years ago, the droughts of the Medieval Warm Period were more severe but the fires less so because of continual surface burning that saved the mature trees from the devastation of crown fire, an "understory burning" that we have suppressed in modern times. In a Colorado cave, a packrat midden reveals the bones and teeth of ancestral voles a million years old that packrats once killed, evidence of an evolving species that suggests a whole flux of climate change, glacial and warming, because of the earth's spin or its axis or the shape of its orbit. We think.

I think of my daughter and her classmates in this last summer of fire, when men and women died in their cars, in their own homes, disbelieving the encroaching flames; when lightning struck Flagstaff mountain, burning toward Upper Skunk Canyon and I feared for my daughter—their dipping the small mammals into fluorescent powder and releasing them to the chaotic dark, their frenetic orbits shining through the tinder grass.

★ ★ ★

"Somebody should shake the eggs," my mother says. I look at her. "In the dark, so the neighbors can't see. Just give them a little shake." She laughs and I am glad to see it, her sadness the trace fossil I fear I'll carry with me. Later, when Leonard and I drive past the lakeside geese, an influx of migration, I have been told, because of global warming, I tell him what my mother says, "Just shake the eggs."

There's a minute of silence, Leonard thinking, and then, bird lover, global warming prophet, Love, he pulls his hands from the steering wheel, slaps them over his face. "Oh god! Oh god!"

★ ★ ★

The Tibetan monks say that to have a mandala there must be one to view it, a "you" to enter the "beauty of perfection" that is the Buddha's mind.

I no longer sweep the porch bare. Instead, Leonard and I leave out apple cores and wilted dinner salad, strewing them all over the snow-stiffened cinquefoil I transplanted alongside the cabin porch in shovelfuls last fall, my mouth bitter with ash and smoke that finally the spare winter snows have quelled. I won't tell my mother this when I walk out with her again, arm in arm, into this prophetic world of ice and fire that already she grieves, change the only impending certainty we know. What will it finally matter, I ask myself, that we fed a packrat who set up housekeeping beneath our porch? Or that we didn't catch it? Or didn't shoot it? On occasion, and only in the most forgiving, anonymous dark, Leonard and I leave crumpled slips of Reynolds Wrap on the bluebird welcome mat like a constellation of origami stars that all night we dream in circles. Our windows still closed for winter, our nocturnal packrat wends its way around and around the stone walls of our cabin, our proxy, as I see it now, a little god we can live with, piling our porch with its pinecones and needles while the first spring catkins of our aspen blow free, these traces preserved.

Birds and Nietzsche

Only the perishable can be beautiful. —Wallace Stevens

I don't know how I saw the bird or knew it different from the understory of these woods beneath our Nipple Mountain, that altricial bluebird, hatchling blind and featherless, "nest hugger" I've heard it called, blown down by July's monsoons into leaf mat, into what each summer we watched turned back to earth.

Nietzsche said truth is a "mobile army of metaphors," and so that day I took you down the southern draw to the aspen shoot to search out the tree scars of a young bear the dogs had frightened the day before, and we followed the curling barbed wire that some vanished rancher had long ago hammered into the living trees as if boundaries could be delineated here, everything was already the litter of a long married season: the scattered branches, whole trees down, "windthrows," the bark barely snagged to the naked boles, and the sapwood long turned to rigid heartwood and its rings.

And then quick light hit the bird, or there was no light, and so I could see its lightness like the skin of an infant, like the too early skin of our premature daughters we once wept over, fearing touch—a skein of touch that could pull the heart out. And then this bird, this warm sac of bird, amidst the linear trees and the hard rocks we called our own.

Why here? Why now? I remember asking you, and how hard I feared I'd become, touching the bird, its head pulling back at my touch, its wide beak opened, insistent against the decay, against the coldness of long rains, the coming dark that would surely kill it, and me saying to you, "Let it stay. Let it die."

★ ★ ★

How little I understood my own parents' or your parents' long marriage when I was younger, the mysteries of familiarity, of love tempered by the body's small failings, everywhere the quiet little deaths, the little angers until finally we would ask ourselves, *where the tenderness like succor?*

Last night, restless in the three o'clock din of the world, in the lonely maelstroms of this changing woman's body, I thought about birds again, of you, of how many years you have slept so quietly here beside me, and of the baby bird, just white space here, but the quiet already moving back into it as wind moves into the trees.

I didn't want to bother finding a box, to feed it sugar water. This is the way of the world, I told you. And so I used a screwdriver to scrape skeleton after skeleton out of our abandoned winter wren house, to show you layer upon layer of baby birds, whole seasons of them like tiny sails of skin and bone. And now I hear the sound of my mother, widowed for years, weeping, her door closed to me still. And your mother, speaking your father's name, *where is Paul*, each day after like a psalm.

Nietzsche calls thoughts "the shadows of feelings—obscurer, emptier, simpler," and so I give you now the sparrow we once found before we were married, its breast impaled by a single thorn, its caught bones floating in the wind, how we let it hang from the bushes months, scoured and beautiful, as we lay in each other's arms for the first time night after night, as if taboo or sacred.

★ ★ ★

There is something of a love poem here, what I had forgotten. You asked me when I knew what love was and I thought of the mountain bluebird, migratory and paired, which flies across the borders of whole countries, season after season, to reach the same nest like this one beneath the eaves of our porch, each dawn the waiting male singing his mate home.

We walked down the south side of our land, that little circle of wilderness we steward, our neighbors shooting at their rusty farm machinery, their bullets pinging back at me over the draw, and you standing at the spring, quieting me, telling me not to shout out at the neighbors, not to shout out at the wind.

And then I found the bird.

No, you said, take it with us, and so I scooped it up with my hand, what I would have embraced as a young girl, let it tumble into my palm, fearful for its bruisings. It opened its beak again and I wrapped it in my shirt, walked the path home behind you, its weight in my hand, its warmth I kept feeling for, circle of our woods evolving, devolving.

Here is my image of you: standing on our precarious rocking chair, me steadying it, and you rolling the naked bird so lightly from your fingers into the hollow bowl of that nest. And how we stood there beneath a half dying tree, my mother looking through the door window, watching us as we waited in wonder to see the bluebird with the whole sky on its back hop from branch to branch, then disappear beneath the porch eaves, a bright bee pinned in its beak.

It was you who first taught me of Nietzsche, who said, "That

for which we find words is something already dead in our hearts,"
and so I won't say the word to you here, now, but know it is in
the caesura of this poem I am giving you when some weeks later
you dragged a footstool from the tool shed so you could check
for the baby bluebird we had left in the care of this other mother.

You put your finger so carefully into the nest.

Here, you said. Then placed a pale blue egg in the hollow of
my hand.

Bathing

In forty-five years since I was a young child bathed by my mother, I have taken I think exactly five baths. Most have been this past year in a claw foot tub my husband and I hauled up Rainbow Pass to this cabin in the shadow of Nipple Mountain where longhorns still linger at the brink of old prospecting glory holes. It's not that I don't understand the need to purify the body: the dark stain of consciousness still flowering out of the old garden, out of the old wounds, Eve the rib fleshed and wanting. I have stood at the mouth of ancient baths in underground ruins, know of the ritual Mikvah baths of my husband's Judaic heritage—lover, bride, menstruating wife, all the grieving who have placed their hands on the newly dead, equally impure and so immersed in the living waters of springs and deep groundwater wells. It's simply that I did not bathe.

In Ohio, when I was thirteen, we lived on a farm behind a cemetery where the metal hulls of parked cars glinted beneath the moon, where high school lovers swam into each other above the soft and dented graves, mornings the damp grass I wept over littered with their beer bottles and spent balloons. Here the Catholic milk farmers raised their sons and daughters in long barrack rooms, ate meals on heavy wood tables longer than caskets, swam naked to cleanse themselves in summer cow ponds. I remember the daughters of the cemetery caretaker who bathed in metal horse troughs with the well water they heated on the kitchen stove, carried steaming into loafing sheds sagging beneath the weight of their long winters. In our house of brick and stone behind farm fences and locked gates, half-built in the years of the Civil War above vanished pig yards and filled with ghosts my mother sometimes heard, voices of those dead farmers passing idly beneath our bay windows, I took my daily showers like a confessional in bathrooms of tile and indoor plumbing.

I sit in water pumped from an aquifer some four hundred and sixty-five feet below me where I imagine the calcified bones of thirsty dinosaurs must rest. Outside the window, jets cruise over me, weave the sky with their white contrails above this mountain plain where once miners washed in the phantom springs I've named. Before the well, before this cabin, we had no real water, bringing the little we could in small coolers when we camped out dirty and ashy, the wild din of coyotes crowding us from the far valley, the summer stars, above our small fires, blurred.

I will tell you I did not bathe because I am almost 5'10", because I don't have the body for it—my knees awkwardly splayed above the water since I was an adolescent. I will tell you I did not bathe because I've never had the predilection for it—the words of my mother, a shower pragmatist, filling me with disdain for the lingering dirt of my own body. I will tell you I did not bathe because I grew up guilty as this "landed gentry"—my father, a successful doctor in a wealthy suburb of Cincinnati, moving us to those cow ponds and horse troughs, to those dirt roads named for the grog once brewed in prohibition stills rusting now in fields and creek beds—and bounded by such resentful poverty. What I won't tell you is that I never loved my body enough.

Once I read that young victims of rape will sometimes go through a stage of promiscuity. I think of the lonely, vulnerable, adolescent girl I was listening beneath the kitchen window to her parents discussing their concern that she wasn't "over it yet," this girl the one ghost my mother could not hear. In Ohio, I sometimes swam naked with the Catholic girls. They didn't like me, but they came anyway to swim in our spring-fed pond, to shed their suits at our sand shores, half-hidden by the weeping willows. I remember covering myself with shamed hands while a birthmark, like the whole of a virginal country I had left long ago, stained unembarrassed the pelvis of the prettiest girl I wished to be. It seems you live your whole life beneath a bruise, and though you push it down, anything can bring it back—an unexpected glimpse at a science study you are too afraid to follow up on, the words of a girl you hear who asks, "Why would anyone want to rape her?" When the Catholic girls stepped into the water, I watched their backs skim the surface like new pennies, this, a baptism I could not receive.

I crack the window open, the moon a thumbnail now, and the earth gone flat beneath the night snow. My own breathing rocks me. I imagine the motion of my mother walking, her belly full with the weight of me rising and falling, the sound of her voice through the placental waters. Even in this tiny amount of bath water, my hands want to lift into the air, swell out of the water like the pale fish at dusk that swam with me those summer nights I was so alone, insects cratering the small moon of my sinking body. Into my twenties, I could count the men in my life on two hands, their bodies slipping finally and always just past me below the stilled waters. For a while I forgot, that thirteenth year disappearing unnoticed, until I saw the weak frail sex of my premature daughters, my mother holding them beneath the kitchen tap to cleanse them because I could not, afraid to touch their nakedness, afraid to touch their fragile skin still flushed with those thimblefuls of my own blood. I think of them now at seventeen, of the stranger who stared at them on the light rail, finally mouthing the word "beautiful" to them before he stepped off, how long they waited for this, the moment when a girl suddenly realizes her own beauty, comes into the whole body of it, and the world awakens to her. I sat next to them, beaten in that florescent light, remembering too, though I never realized that moment, never.

The dog pushes his long delicate snout through the cracked door. He cries and whimpers. I pull the plug and step out of the water, bath bubbles clinging to me. In the dim mirror, my body is a study of shadow and light. I think it was made to be seen against the warmth of cabin wood, the knots and linear waves of Douglas fir, the brown tones of it melding into the long grain the air darkens, all the voices finally gone. Tonight I will sleep on the couch in front of the woodstove where the aspen stump I dug out of the drifts cracks and burns. The wind sings through the window like a siren, and the steam floats from my skin like thin milk.

Disjunctions of Lichen

In the artist of all kinds, one can detect an inherent dilemma . . .
the urgent need to communicate and the still more urgent need
not to be found. —D.W. Winicott

Of course, I love the names: *dog pelt, hooded bone, blistered rock-
tripe, shadow ruffle.* What poet's soul named them before scientific
observation and laboratory extraction, before their Latinate?
Who thought to feed the wolf the poisoned one mixed with
splintered glass, to tip the killing stone arrow with it, to name
it *wolf bane?* I meant to write of lichen today, to do the math
that separates its Devonian fossils of four hundred million years
with our Quaternary fossils of two hundred thousand years,
to confess the eight I blindly stepped on, sat on, stood on this
hundred years' welding of wedded fungus and algae. Unwitting
disperser—*it does not prevent us from requiring the unpredictable
beauty of disjunction*—I have broken from brecciate rock delicate
powder, ruffled leaf, hollow tube smaller than the cuttings of
my fingernail to the endless wind and never known it.

But there are great migrations here—our mild winter at fault,
my Mephistopheles husband reminds me who does not want to
believe in global warming. In winter, the animals and I live so

vicariously, so segmented. I know so many only by sound—elk bugle on a far rise, owl hoot stoic in the pine. Or I know them by scat: hair and bone fragments, curve of field mice teeth enclosed in owl pellet, twisted tubular cords of waste gray with the hair of what coyote has eaten, mule deer pellets buried dark and fresh beneath the snow. Or I know them by what they cache: the frozen rabbit, partially eaten in the snow at the base of a tree—a mountain lion's catch the poodle keeps trying to choke down whole as I hang onto a thawed and bloody foot, the whole time thinking—*wakes the bitter memory/Of what he was, what is, and what must be*—of the snake on my father's Ohio farm swallowing before my eyes a toad whole, whole body of the snake distending, muscling the toad through, and the toad, word, dissolving.

This morning, in every aspen tree, hang the white tents of caterpillars that will eat the leaves from the stems, and I batter them to the ground. What killing is this? Like the seasonal cluster flies Leonard swears I will soon bite out of the air and spit between my teeth? Or the skeletal nestlings I found too late in the winter wren house I hung from a branch, all spring the wind knocking those frail bones to death? Last winter—*when each step/backward is a step/downward, when what you move toward moves toward/you*—I walked out into it, snow in the woods, clouds pushing up from the valley, Nipple Mountain, the trees, me in shrouds, and only the yellow grass visible. And then I heard a car horn sounding far off, honking one beat at a time, and I wondered if someone had fallen into a ditch. It was clearly a calling out. Birds roosted in the thickest fir trees—sparrows and the small winter wrens I thought I had killed—and I heard a hollow knocking high in the trees, a half branch somewhere split off and hanging, but I couldn't see it, though I looked and looked, stood still in the snow, listened for quiet everywhere.

Last night I slept beneath the wings of *Noctuidae*—miller moth, owlet moth, army cutworm moth drawn through the window cracks to my reading lamp. Not just one or two but dozens, erratic, fevered by light. I plucked them one by one from the air, tossed them diapausal, eggless, back into the night, more and more descending out of the shadows, twirling above me like dreams or words, nouns and predicates I understand I might never speak, *witch's hair, ragged paperdoll,* until finally there was nothing but darkness and sleep to give into, my tired, yes, poet hands—*for a moment I forget who I am and where I am*— all night slick with their wing dust.

Heresies of the Holy

I stretch an aspen leaf, mottled, rotting, moist with the vanishing hail and snow of last night between my thumbs and forefingers. Some twenty thousand years ago, our primitive ancestors blew into the hollowed bones of the dead, or across the stems of plants they could bore into with their stones, and heard, for the first time, the holy voices conjured into being with their own breath, a manifestation of the spiritual world the men found so transforming that if a woman—I have read this—were to touch such instruments of the gods, she would be strangled. Or poisoned.

Early winter morning beneath Nipple Mountain, the rutting season of the wapiti, "White rumps," what the Indians named the elk that range past our cabin in altitudinal migrations. I want to say what Thoreau said: "The morning wind forever blows, the poem of creation . . . uninterrupted." But last night I read the poems of grieving from a woman I knew when I was barely twenty-one, a poet I was in awe of, ten years my senior, a woman who this year climbed at the age of sixty to the top of an East Coast football stadium and jumped. And I wondered why, this death neither good nor swift, and I thought of her leaning back in her chair that one day far ago at a writer's workshop in Iowa, stretching her young and beautiful body through the air as if it moved through water, freed from gravity or weight, and how my then-lover, who would soon scorn me, watched her breasts swell beneath her white sweater with so much longing.

This morning, exhausted, filled with something nameless, I heard the bull elks bugling across the valley. Fog, low clouds, the dark mottled gold of aspen leaves half in air, half on ground, and the mountain grass stiff and bleached with this new frost, I followed the old cow trails to stand here above the valley where a dark swallow of Douglas fir stretches down from the granite boulders that hold me.

What is grief? Or more specifically, an aging woman's grief?

A Navajo once told me that if a menstruating woman nears a man who has pierced himself in dance, his blood flowing too, she interrupts his communion with the spirit world, and so must leave. And though my husband's Jewish family has never said this to me, I know that in the Book of Leviticus, a menstruating woman is considered *niddah*—a term of "separation," of "ritual impurity,"—and, thus, untouchable even to her husband.

Unclean, the Bible says, *if her flowers be upon him* until the white cloth of the Hebrew *eid* she wipes herself with stays unsullied for seven days after.

Flowers. Menses. *Life-essence,* the prehistorics called in wonder the letting of this *wise blood,* the only time human blood sheds "without wounding," they said. And *Adam.* The word comes from the ancient Mesopotamia term, *adamah,* "bloody clay," or "red earth" of the woman's body.

Yet I remember the shame of my daughter when she was young and her menstrual blood spilled strong and unexpectedly when she was riding her bike blocks from our home. This blood that cycles with the moon—if no artificial light disrupts the rhythms of the body, the woman bleeds on the dark of the moon, and, on the full, ripens, her eggs bursting from her ovaries into primordial existence. But even then, in a woman's reproductive prime, when she is most in sync with nature and man, it seems she is cast out again and again from the spiritual world, whether it be native or modern. In Emerson's essay, "Nature"—though, yes, it can be argued this is a matter of nineteenth century convention—it is man whom "a wild delight runs through" in the presence of nature, man whom the "currents of the Universal Being" washes through, man who is "part or particle of God."

Not woman. Man, Adam, through whom the Bible says, *death entered all.*

Wordsworth said it is impossible to speak of grief or loneliness when you are in the grip of it. Better to speak of it in that tranquility recollected. I think it was my mother who said that when a woman gets to be of a "certain age," she is ignored. My mother, beset monthly by menstrual cycles that left her bed-ridden when she was a young girl, a legacy of an almost folkloric ancestor who hemorrhaged to death in her bed, bearer of some estrogenic gene gone haywire that I fear I have inherited, source of this endless, meandering, premenopausal sojourn—what my mother promises me will last until I am fifty-three, "at least."

I remember when I was young, the men who called me "beauty," "angel face." How tenderly in the moon's light they came to me. And the words of this woman poet I am grieving now, though I was nothing to her all the years after I knew her that little while and my lover wanted her so, of the men she said she loved, who loved her, who were unfaithful or to whom she was unfaithful, of those she lost, the scent of their sex in her hair still. When I saw her, a woman of "certain age," widowed, her grown children far from her, reading her poems on some video filmed just weeks before her dying, not once looking up from what she said, I knew her. And I thought of the hours I have spent here where once men disrupted this land for me to build this cabin I love, in this place I love, the hours I have spent crawling on my knees, broadcasting seed over the erupted rock, the seed in my bucket like the fine shells of broken insects or the torn butterflies I've seen crumpled, turning to dust in the steel corners of glass pavilions, the wind lifting this seed out of my bucket, cutting it from my veined hands given me by my deep and dark and, sometimes, sad mother who said when she was fifty, she had nothing.

Did my woman poet know this too?

An elk bugles now, a sound strangled, hoarse, desperate. Behind me, the starving longhorns left too long on these early winter meadows bawl back in answer. Why am I drawn to this lonely place of cattle herds and elk and coyote I seldom hear now? My husband says I am a lover of landscapes, not of people. Perhaps this is why I come here so often, though once someone said to me only those who are depressed seek such solitude, as if a woman's venturing into the vestiges of wilderness could not be thought "pilgrimage."

Once, I went to the baptism of a smooth-brained baby, victim of a genetic disorder in which the un-creased cerebral cortex does not allow human thought beyond the reflexes of the larval body. The child would die in its infancy. We gathered in an old Lutheran church filled with the relics of Jesus—his splayed body on the cross, his cross engraved upon the thick wax candles, upon the brass bowls filled with his holy water, Christ and his saints stained in the early morning light above us.

Baptism, the priest told us, cleanses the sin of first man from the soul as water touches the body, the child flourishing into the communion of man, the communion of the holy, this the gift of the Holy Spirit, its tangible symbol of what is intangible.

The Seven Sacraments say, *but even a layman or woman, nay, even a pagan or heretic can baptize,* and I remember watching this mother—equated by the Bible as if to some lower order of being—nursing, beatific; this child, this blind unthinking creature, with the holy waters of herself while the priest spoke; this priest never once getting it right, this grieving, or this living, this wake for the dead, or for the dying, like a river women enter wholly, nakedly, this mother's weeping, when she did, I think, guttural, wordless, the real Mourner's Kaddish of my husband's faith.

I found the skull of a hawk on these rocks once, what I know my slightly pantheistic mother would love, and what I like to think my dead woman poet might have liked, too. I waited months for the sun and the wind and the rain to hone it white as alabaster against the dark hook of its hawk beak, so I might save it like a relic on the dark shelf of the holy. But sometimes I fear we fictionalize our lives so willingly, see what we want to, and then, suddenly, we are given such searing moments of reality, and even then we are not sure of what is truth, or merely grief, or the vagrancies of an aging body.

Even here, in this place I think holy, my neighbors fence their land and warn me of prosecution for my trespasses. I stumble over scat and elk droppings and the long bones of steers. I have no God. I am no man nor Thoreau nor Emerson. I am an aging woman, like this woman poet I once knew, a half-menopausal woman in a field full of dull barbed wire, where desperate cattle trample down the muddy leaks of a spring to drink in the drought of this winter, and where micro bursts of wind slay whole stands of trees, and people I do not know throw their trash and mattress springs into these glory holes I love.

And I carry the poems of a dead woman inside me.

One early evening, a deer strayed from the woods to the east across the meadow behind our cabin. The *emissaries of the gods*, the ancient Celtics called the deer, leading the chosen into the realm of the spiritual, of the fleshless. I could barely see the deer through the glass, all curves against the straight and crooked angles of the aspen trees, its rack of antlers, its velvet a softness of light in the early dark. It grazed in the native grass and wild-flowers I finally hired some day-laborer to sow into the rocks. Then the lights in the cabin began to take over the glass doors— fire of the wood stove, silhouette of myself. I startled. Within my face, within my mirrored body, stood the deer, quiet, star-ing back. Did he see my small, frightened movements, the light rocking of my body gathering air? He stepped closer, and we stared between the porch railings at each other, cusp of deer and woman, cusp of what is holy and what is not, until the inevita-ble darkness.

My woman poet stares down that last moment from her stadium as I do now from this high, lonely place. I think of those prim-itive men some twenty thousand years ago and of the skull of the hawk I once held with my woman's hands against the clear sky. I stretch the aspen leaf between my fingers, tighter now: the reed of a flute, of anything, I think, that sings beyond this human world. I blow into it, blow again and again, badly, like a woman who has waited her whole life to claim what is holy. Tiny spurts of sound, and then, finally, a clear high blast of my breath vibrating the leaf.

Silence. Silence.

And then an elk bugles and five appear over the ridge, stand listening to me. Then a river of elk—fifty, seventy—pound across the clearing, disappear into the trees, the bull elk left standing, bugling back to my small high blasts, wild along the stone ridges.

Notes

André Kertész Distortion #40 Gelatin silver print. 1933.
© Estate of André Kertész/Higher Pictures

Quotes from the "Homeric Hymn 2 to Demeter" come from the Internet Sacred Text Archive.

Homer, Hymn to Demeter, trans. Hugh G. Evelyn-White, Internet Sacred Text Archive, http://www.sacred-texts.com/cla/demeter.htm

Quotes from "Galileo" come from the following sources:

"Simple Motion of Descent" comes from

   Galileo Galilei, *Dialogue on the Great World Systems*, ed. revised. Giorgio De Santillana (Chicago,1953), 177.

"It is impossible that anything should have" comes from

   Roberto Torretti, *Creative Understanding* (Chicago: University of Chicago Press, 2010), 45.

Quotes from "On White Space and Silence" come from the following sources:

Robert Bly, " A Wrong Turning in American Poetry," in *American Poetry: Wildness and Domesticity* (New York: Harper-Perennial, 1990), 13.

Kim Barnes, "Interview." *Creative Nonfiction: A Guide and Anthology*, Eds Bradway and Hesse (Boston: Bedford/ St. Martin, 2009), 202.

Kevin Bushell, "Leaping Into the Unknown: The Poetics of Robert Bly's Deep Image," *Modern American Poetry*, http://www.english.illinois.edu/maps/poets/a_f/bly/bushell.html.

Barnes, "Interview," 203.

Bly, "Wrong Turning," 63.

James Longenbach, *The Art of the Poetic Line* (Saint Paul: Graywolf Press, 2008).

Changing Minds. org, "Signified and Signifier," http://changingminds.org/explanations/criti-cal_theory/concepts/signifier_signified.htm.

Rainier Maria Rilke, "The Second Elegy," in *The Selected Poetry of Rainier Maria Rilke* (New York: Vintage, 1982).

Quotes from "Disjunctions of Lichen":

"it does not prevent us . . . disjunction"

John Longenbach, *The Resistance to Poetry* (Chicago: University of Chicago Press, 2005), 133.

"wakes the bitter memory of . . . what must be "

John Milton, *Paradise Lost: Book IV*, Poetry Foundation, http://www.poetryfoundation.org/poem/174004.

"when each step . . . moves toward you"

Frank Bidart, "The Second Hour of the Night" in *Desire* (New York: Farrar, Straus and Giroux Paperbacks, 1999).

"for a moment I forget . . .and where I am"

Primo Levi, *If This Is A Man And A Truce* (New York: Little, Brown Group, 1991).

Acknowledgments

Pieces in this collection have appeared, sometimes in different form, in the following publications. Many thanks to those who published my work:

"Bear of My Girlhood" originally "Mother Like Me," *Natural Homes Magazine*

"Speaking the Word," *The Denver Post*

"Heresies of the Holy," "Bathing," and "Middens" *Fourth Genre*

"Of Wind and Fire" upcoming, *The Florida Review*

"The Winter Garden," *The Herb Companion*

"Phantom Mares" and "Guns, Knives and the Amazon Princess Warrior," *Hotel Amerika*

"Talismans of the Whirlpool," *Literary Mama*

"On White Space and Silence," *Puerto del Sol*

"Unearthing *Leetso*," *River Teeth*

"Disjunction of Lichen," *Talking Writing: A magazine for writers*"

"Dark Skies," and "Finding the Well," *Wazee Online Journal*

"Heresies of the Holy" was a finalist for Fourth Genre's 2011 Michael Steinberg Essay Prize

"Wind and Fire" was a finalist for Fourth Genre's 2012 Michael Steinberg Essay Prize and semi-finalist for the Florida Review Editors' Award.

"Bathing" was named a notable essay in the 2011 Best American Essays. It has been reprinted in the 6th edition of *The Fourth Genre: Contemporary Writers of/an Creative Nonfiction* textbook/anthology.

Many thanks to all of those who have helped me on the journey of creating this book. Particular thanks to Annie Dawid, Robert Root, Steve Harvey, Jill Christman, and Liz Netzel. Thanks to all of my colleagues at Ashland University's MFA program for their support and inspiration. Thanks to Lindsay Lewan and Lucy Graca, my colleagues at Arapahoe Community College, for their support and friendship. Gratitude to my editors and publishers, Sonya Unrein and Caleb Seeling, for their skills and insights. Love always to Leonard, my first true reader, my girls, my mother, my family.

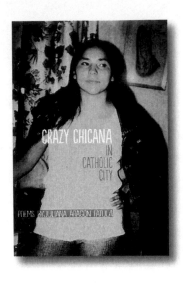

CRAZY CHICANA IN CATHOLIC CITY

Poems by JULIANA ARAGON FATULA

"Juliana Aragon Fatula writes histories so terrifying they feel as if they were written with a knife. She writes with craft and courage about what most folks are too ashamed to even think about, let along talk about. Her fearlessness is inspirational. This is the kind of poetry I want to read; this is the kind I want to write."

—SANDRA CISNEROS

AVAILABLE IN PAPERBACK AND EBOOK

MORE GREAT BOOKS FROM CONUNDRUM PRESS

MEMORY'S ROOMS

Poems by ELEANOR SWANSON

"More than a simple book of poetry, Eleanor Swanson has created a living scrapbook. As we turn the pages each memory snapshot bursts into life, from sepia tones to brilliant bouquets of words.

"She doesn't just write about beauty; indeed the poem that has remained with me for days is beautiful and powerful, but not about beauty at all."

—STORY CIRCLE BOOKS

AVAILABLE IN PAPERBACK